T0286795

Cambridge Elements ≡

Elements in Political Economy
edited by
David Stasavage
New York University

REFORM AND REBELLION IN WEAK STATES

Evgeny Finkel
Johns Hopkins University

Scott Gehlbach
The University of Chicago

CAMBRIDGE
UNIVERSITY PRESS

CAMBRIDGE
UNIVERSITY PRESS

University Printing House, Cambridge CB2 8BS, United Kingdom

One Liberty Plaza, 20th Floor, New York, NY 10006, USA

477 Williamstown Road, Port Melbourne, VIC 3207, Australia

314–321, 3rd Floor, Plot 3, Splendor Forum, Jasola District Centre, New Delhi – 110025, India

79 Anson Road, #06–04/06, Singapore 079906

Cambridge University Press is part of the University of Cambridge.

It furthers the University's mission by disseminating knowledge in the pursuit of education, learning, and research at the highest international levels of excellence.

www.cambridge.org
Information on this title: www.cambridge.org/9781108796477
DOI: 10.1017/9781108855112

© Evgeny Finkel and Scott Gehlbach 2020

First published 2020

A catalogue record for this publication is available from the British Library.

ISBN 978-1-108-79647-7 Paperback
ISSN 2398-4031 (Online)
ISSN 2514-3816 (Print)

Reform and Rebellion in Weak States

Elements in Political Economy

DOI: 10.1017/9781108855112
First published online: May 2020

Evgeny Finkel
Johns Hopkins University
Scott Gehlbach
The University of Chicago
Author for correspondence: Scott Gehlbach, gehlbach@uchicago.edu

Abstract: Throughout history, reform has provoked rebellion – not just by the losers from reform, but also among its intended beneficiaries. In *Reform and Rebellion in Weak States*, Evgeny Finkel and Scott Gehlbach emphasize that reform often must be implemented by local actors with a stake in the status quo. In this setting, the promise of reform represents an implicit contract against which subsequent implementation is measured: when implementation falls short of this promise, citizens are aggrieved and more likely to rebel. Finkel and Gehlbach explore this argument in the context of Russia's emancipation of the serfs in 1861 – a fundamental reform of Russian state and society that paradoxically encouraged unrest among the peasants who were its prime beneficiaries. They further examine the empirical reach of their theory through narrative analyses of the Tanzimat reforms of the nineteenth-century Ottoman Empire, land reform in ancient Rome, the abolition of feudalism during the French Revolution, and land reform in contemporary Latin America.

Keywords: reform, rebellion, weak states, Russia, Ottoman Empire, ancient Rome, French Revolution, Latin America

ISBNs: 9781108796477 (PB), 9781108855112 (OC)
ISSNs: 2398-4031 (online), 2514-3816 (print)

Contents

1 Introduction

> The regime that a revolution destroys is almost always better than the one
> that immediately preceded it, and experience teaches that the most dangerous
> time for a bad government is usually when it begins to reform.
>
> Alexis de Tocqueville (2011 [1856], p. 157)

As we write these words, the world seems engulfed in protest. Across France, hundreds of thousands of "Yellow Jackets" take to the streets to protest hikes in gasoline taxes and the broader economic agenda of President Macron, who "is once again finding that the French do not respond well to reform."[1] In Jordan, seventeen people are arrested in protests against a fiscal reform and new tax law that raises taxes on citizens and businesses – this, after an earlier, much larger wave of disturbances that shook the monarchy in June 2018. Protest activities in Russia more than tripled in the third quarter of 2018, compared to the beginning of the year (Tsentr Ekonomicheskikh i Politicheskikh Reform, 2018), as citizens responded to a government plan to raise the retirement age. Protests against tax reform in Costa Rica turned violent in September 2018, while in neighboring Nicaragua the government was forced to cancel welfare system reforms after a wave of deadly disturbances. And in Madison, Wisconsin, protesters once again converged on the state capitol – this time in response to legislation sponsored by Republican lawmakers that would (and ultimately did) reduce the powers of the incoming Democratic governor and attorney general.

A casual observer would find it easy to understand these events. Faced with threats to their rights and economic well-being, the losers from reform turn out in protest. A scholar steeped in the literature on contentious politics might dig deeper, asking whether changes in the political opportunity structure or other factors had facilitated protest at this time and place – but he or she would likely also treat the underlying grievances as intuitive.

Yet as suggested by the epigraph that begins this Element, there are numerous instances of contentious political action where those who rebel are the intended winners, not losers, from reform. As we show in the following pages, the emancipation of serfs in Russia led to increased unrest among precisely those peasants. Similarly, the abolition of feudalism in revolutionary France increased, not decreased, unrest in the French countryside. The end of tax farming in the Ottoman Empire provoked disturbances among those who stood to benefit. Land redistribution in ancient Rome arguably contributed to the

---

[1] Smith, Saphora. "Who are France's 'Yellow Jacket' protesters and what do they want?" NBC News, November 27, 2018.

outbreak of the Social War between Rome and its Italian allies. And land reform in twentieth-century Columbia, Peru under Fernando Belaúnde Terry, and Chile under Eduardo Frei Montalva all encouraged unrest among peasants and workers on agricultural estates.

Nonetheless, as these same cases illustrate, reform sometimes promotes rather than undermines social stability. Roman (as opposed to non-Roman Italian) citizens who were targeted for benefits under the *Lex Sempronia Agraria* of Tiberius Gracchus appear not to have rebelled. The same is true of the peasants who gained land through reform in Costa Rica, Bolivia, and Peru under Juan Velasco Alvarado.

1.1 Understanding Reform and Rebellion

When does reform provoke rebellion among its intended beneficiaries, and when does it discourage it? To answer this question, we present a theory that emphasizes that reform often must be implemented by local actors with a stake in the status quo. In this setting, the promise of reform represents an implicit contract against which subsequent implementation is measured: when implementation falls short of this promise, citizens are aggrieved and more likely to rebel.

Together, these assumptions imply that when – for reasons of state capacity or the nature of reform – the implementation of reform is predominantly local, a more ambitious reform leads to greater disappointment and thus more unrest. Notably, this is true even though rebellion is costly for the local elites responsible for carrying out reform. Conversely, when the implementation of reform is largely under central control, then grievances and hence rebellion are decreasing in the extent of reform.

This theory helps to make sense of the diverse outcomes we explore in subsequent sections. For most of the cases we examine, reform was substantially delegated to local elites. In Russia, for example, the central state was far too weak to implement reform on its own. With little state presence outside of provincial capitals, the tsar and his ministers had no choice but to rely on the nobility – the very landowners who stood to lose from reform – to carry out the redistribution of land rights and renegotiation of obligations that were central to emancipation. When the implementation of reform inevitably drifted from its stated intent, former serfs rebelled.

For a few of the cases we examine, however, reform was centrally rather than locally implemented. A legacy of land redistribution in ancient Rome enabled a top-down land reform that targeted Roman citizens. In Bolivia, land reform was similarly guided by a central commission dominated by supporters of reform. Here and elsewhere, the implementation of reform largely lived up to its promise, encouraging social stability.

1.2 The Tocqueville Paradox in the Literature

Our analysis builds on Alexis de Tocqueville's intuition that reforms present a danger to the regime that undertakes them. While at odds with many contemporary models of political economy that are neatly encapsulated by Adam Przeworski's observation that "extensions of rights are a response of the incumbent holders of rights to revolutionary threats by the excluded" (Przeworski, 2009, p. 292),[2] Tocqueville's paradoxical conjecture has served as a basis for numerous earlier contributions.[3]

A common interpretation of Tocqueville's argument is that reforms lead to rising, but rarely fulfilled, expectations among citizens. This understanding occupies an important place in Davies's (1962) famous "J-curve" theory of revolution, in which a period of wealth and advancement is followed by backsliding and worsening of conditions, eventually leading to rebellion. Building on Davies, Tocqueville's observation informs Gurr's (1970) theory of relative deprivation, in which expectations of improvement are juxtaposed with a much harsher reality, leading "men" to rebel. The same logic also underlies the work of Huntington (1968, p. 163), where a slightly different translation of Tocqueville's conjecture serves as the basis for the contention that reforms may be a "catalyst" for social instability. A key contribution of our theoretical perspective is to clarify why expectations are so often unmet.

Beyond these general arguments, the Tocqueville paradox has been used by scholars to account for particular cases of large-scale social unrest. Thus, for example, Grieder (2012, pp. 37–38) relies on Tocqueville to explain the 1953 riots in East Germany, where, following Stalin's death, a "New Course" was announced by communist elites. Similarly, Dubow (2014, p. 205) argues that Tocqueville's logic helps to explain the crisis of legitimacy that followed the apartheid-era South African government's initial power-sharing reforms.

An alternative interpretation of the Tocqueville paradox is that reforms create an opening for collective action. This view is most explicitly articulated by

---

[2] See, for example, Acemoglu and Robinson (2000, 2001, 2006); Boix (2003); Gandhi and Przeworski (2006); Dunning (2008); Ansell and Samuels (2010); Svolik (2012); Miller (2013).

[3] A related body of work (Acemoglu et al., 2018; Healy et al., 2017) considers Tocqueville's varying conjectures about the relationship between social mobility – that is, the possibility of moving up or down the income distribution – and social stability (de Tocqueville, 2002 [1835/40], 2011 [1856]).

Tarrow (1989), who uses Tocqueville in positing the role of political opportunity structure in contentious action. Tarrow (2011) again draws the analogy, suggesting that changes to political opportunity structure can explain momentous events such as the collapse of the USSR. "How could so massive a wave of political contention develop in so centralized a regime after decades of repression? The simplest answer was provided by Alexis de Tocqueville . . . Had he been present two hundred years later, he might well have applied his theory to the Soviet Union" (Tarrow, 2011, p. 157).

An inevitable limitation of these perspectives is that they present a rather singular relationship between reform and social unrest. Tocqueville himself seemed to largely share this view, writing that "[o]nly a great genius can save a ruler who is setting out to relieve his subjects' suffering after a long period of oppression" (de Tocqueville, 2008 [1856], p. 175). Whereas genius might certainly play a role, later scholarship does identify conditions under which reforms might not lead to unrest. Most relevant for our perspective is the work of Bertrand (2013) and Haggard and Kaufman (1992, 1995), who argue that strong state institutions reduce the likelihood of substantial pressure from below in the wake of reforms.[4]

A final line of argument takes structural factors as given and focuses instead on reform's design. Evidence from East Asia suggests that, when implemented slowly and cautiously, reforms might not lead to massive social instability and danger to the regime (Bertrand, 2013; Dimitrov, 2013) – an argument with echoes in the literature on the normative political economy of reform (Dewatripont and Roland, 1992, 1995). The model that we present in the following section deals with such considerations in reduced-form manner by parameterizing the scale of reform.

1.3 Plan of the Element

This Element is structured as follows. Section 2 presents our theoretical model, from which we derive predictions about the (conditional) relationship between reform and rebellion and various implications for the optimal design of reform. Section 3 explores in detail Russia's emancipation of the serfs in 1861 – an important reform for which we have unusually rich data on peasant unrest and an empirical setting that allows for the identification of a causal effect of reform on rebellion. Section 4 further extends our analysis by briefly discussing the impact of various reforms on social stability in several additional settings: the Tanzimat Reforms of the late Ottoman Empire, the land reform of

---

[4] Numerous models consider mechanisms by which autocrats might reduce the risk of rebellion without explicitly tying unrest to reform. For a review, see Gehlbach et al. (2016).

Tiberius Gracchus in ancient Rome, the abolition of feudalism in the early days of the French Revolution, and various land reforms in twentieth-century Latin America. The final section concludes.

2 Theory

What is the relationship between reform and rebellion? In *The Ancien Régime and the French Revolution*, Alexis de Tocqueville famously argued: "The regime that a revolution destroys is almost always better than the one that immediately preceded it, and experience teaches that the most dangerous time for a bad government is usually when it begins to reform" (de Tocqueville, 2011 [1856], p. 157). Behind this quote lie two ideas: reform may provoke rather than prevent rebellion, and whether it does so depends on the character of the state In this section we present a theory that develops both ideas.

2.1 Building Blocks

Our argument builds on Tocqueville in emphasizing the role of reform in raising expectations that cannot easily be satisfied: "The evil that one endures patiently because it seems inevitable becomes unbearable the moment its elimination becomes conceivable" (de Tocqueville, 2011 [1856], p. 157). But why should the expectations raised by reform be so hard to fulfill? One possibility is that reform, once announced – and expectations raised – can still be blocked by actors with a stake in the status quo. Expressing this view, Oberschall (1995, pp. 155–157) suggests that "Tocqueville's paradox" is in fact hardly surprising, as "reform attempts tend to be half-hearted and ineffective because of institutional weakness and deliberate efforts by certain groups to undermine them." The actual outcome is "erratic reformism," exacerbating rather than quieting discontent.

This perspective, in turn, raises further questions. To what extent do the "certain groups" in a position to block implementation of reform internalize the resulting rebellion? Is there always a trade-off between stability and reform, or is it possible to pursue the latter without risking the former? Finally, is reform indeed most dangerous for what Tocqueville referred to as "bad governments"?

To answer these questions, we develop a simple model of reform and rebellion. Our modeling approach incorporates two key assumptions. First, we assume that some part of reform, modeled simply as the reallocation of a divisible resource, must be *implemented* by a strategic agent – a local elite, in our formalization – with a stake in the status quo. Even autocratic rulers cannot rule by fiat alone but instead must rely upon formal or informal agents to carry out bureaucratically demanding tasks. Those agents with sufficient expertise to implement reform – or sufficient power to block its local implementation – are often those with the most to lose.

An instructive case, which we discuss at length in Section 3, is Russia's emancipation of the serfs in 1861: implementation of this complicated reform was by necessity substantially delegated to the nobility that possessed the land on which serfs resided. More generally, land reform often provides opportunities for obstruction by local elites (Albertus, 2015; Albertus and Kaplan, 2013). When, in the wake of decolonization, numerous African states embarked on heavily "top-down" land reforms, the results were often abysmal. Recognizing these failures, in the early 1990s central states "backed off" and delegated the implementation of land redistribution and titling to local actors (Bruce and Knox, 2009). Such processes also extend to other types of reform. As we discuss in Section 4, when the Ottoman Empire moved from tax farming to direct taxation as part of the mid-nineteenth-century Tanzimat Reforms, it often had to rely on pre-reform tax farmers to implement the change, even though these individuals had everything to lose and almost nothing to gain from the new situation (Aytekın, 2012). Similarly, the Industrial Communities program in Juan Velasco's Peru, which sought to increase worker control and profit sharing in industrial enterprises, could only succeed with the acquiescence of enterprise managers (Stokes, 1995, pp. 33–34). Even the most capacious states often depend on local agents to implement certain reforms. For instance, education reforms typically depend on the conduct of teachers, who are "the final brokers when it comes to implementing policy" in their classrooms (Spillane, 2000, p. 142), regardless of whether they gain or lose from reform.

Our second key assumption is that reform represents an *implicit contract* against which subsequent implementation is measured. To the extent that implementation falls short of the promise of reform, citizens are aggrieved and consequently more likely to rebel. This perspective builds most directly on recent work in economics on contracts as reference points – with the key difference that the contract is imposed upon, rather than negotiated by, the actor responsible for its implementation. As in that literature (see especially Hart and Moore, 2008; Hart and Holmstrom, 2010), we adopt the stark assumption that citizens' aggrievement, and thus propensity to rebel, is increasing in the difference between the maximum they could have received (the promise of reform) and what they actually do (the implementation of reform).

The verisimilitude of this behavioral assumption is plausibly supported by related work on two distinct phenomena. First, a long literature in various disciplines emphasizes that rebellion is driven, at least in part, by "grievances" or "expressive" concerns (e.g., Gurr, 1970; Scott, 1976; Wood, 2003), sometimes in interaction with more instrumental motivations (van Zomeren et al., 2004, 2012; Humphreys and Weinstein, 2008).[5] In our setting, such grievances are driven by disappointment with the implementation of reform. Second, a substantial literature demonstrates the importance across a range of field and laboratory environments of "reference dependence" – that is, the tendency of individuals to "normally perceive outcomes as gains and losses . . . relative to some neutral reference point" (Kahneman and Tversky, 1979, p. 274).[6] We argue that the promise of reform can serve as one such reference point.

As our discussion of the Russian case in Section 3 illustrates, the promise of reform is often quite visible, creating the potential for disappointment – and thus unrest – when the implementation of reform is blocked. Intuitively, we can think of citizens as "endowed" by reform with a share of the contested resource (Thaler, 1980; Knetsch, 1989; Kahneman et al., 1990); the failure of elites to fulfill that promise is experienced as a loss of the endowment.[7] At the same time, such grievances may be at least partially offset to the extent that reform improves on the status quo – another important reference point that is emphasized in some experimental work.[8] Rather than choosing between these two reference points in an ad hoc manner, we parameterize their relative importance. Our key results relate to the weight that citizens place on gains

---

[5] Chong (2014, ch. 4) refers to expressive behavior as noninstrumental but "narrowly rational," which accords with our assumption that such concerns enter the cost-benefit calculation in the decision to rebel. Blattman and Miguel (2010) suggest that the weak statistical evidence for such motivations in some studies may be a consequence of the crude proxies employed, and they call for the development of better measures of grievances. For a formal theory of grievance-based (vs. political-process) contentious politics, see Shadmehr (2014).

[6] For reviews, see Camerer et al. (2004) and DellaVigna (2009). Formal models of political behavior have considered a variety of reference points, including the status quo (Alesina and Passarelli, 2015; Lockwood and Rockey, 2015), the solution to a biased social-welfare maximization problem (Passarelli and Tabellini, 2017), past payoffs (Bendor et al., 2003), rational expectations of future payoffs (Grillo, 2016; Acharya and Grillo, 2017), and aspirations established by parents (Besley, 2016).

[7] The assumption that citizens are more likely to rebel when implementation falls short of the promise of reform can also be motivated by the observation that individuals are willing to take costly actions to punish those who hurt them (Rabin, 1993) and by evidence that collective action is more likely when citizens are able to trace blame to specific, identifiable actors (Javeline, 2003a, b) – in our context, the elites responsible for reform's local implementation.

[8] For discussion, see Kőszegi and Rabin (2006). Our formulation of dual reference points is consistent with the "reference lotteries" in Kőszegi and Rabin if one interprets the status quo and promise of reform as potential outcomes, though our analysis does not invoke that paper's "extreme" (p. 1135) assumption that expectations under this lottery are determined by equilibrium strategies. In a review essay, Bendor (2016) emphasizes that Kahneman and Tversky's (1979) invocation of the status quo as a reference point was an "auxiliary hypothesis" and that different environments may feature different reference points. For discussion and a theoretical framework that employs both aspirations and the status quo as reference points, see Mo (2018).

over the status quo (versus losses from incomplete implementation), relative to the extent to which the implementation of reform is under local (rather than central) control.

2.2 Model

Our behavioral assumptions pin down the probability of unrest, *given* the degree of local implementation. The need for a model is to evaluate the strategic response of local elites, for whom we assume rebellion is costly. Here we present a highly stylized model that abstracts from various considerations. Later in this section and in Finkel and Gehlbach (2018) we discuss robustness of our key results to numerous extensions and generalizations.

Our model takes the form of a bargaining game featuring an *elite* and a *citizenry*, considered as unitary actors. It is useful to think of the elite and citizenry as local actors within a larger polity – an interpretation that we will discuss further.

We are interested in the response of the citizenry to reform $\gamma \in (0, 1]$, where the parameter γ denotes the proportion of an infinitely divisible resource to be transferred from the elite to the citizenry. We do not provide a model of the process by which γ is chosen, though our analysis implies a number of lessons for reform design, which we will discuss. Implicitly, we model the subgame that follows the unmodeled choice of γ by a central government. We let $\hat{\gamma}$ denote the status quo allocation of the resource to the citizenry, where $\hat{\gamma} < \gamma$.

The implementation of reform depends in part on the behavior of the local elite. In particular, we assume exogenous proportion $\lambda \in (0, 1)$ of the resource to be under control of the elite, which chooses a *local implementation* of reform $x \in [0, \gamma]$. In contrast, proportion $(1 - \lambda)\gamma$ is transferred automatically to the citizenry – for example, because an unmodeled central government has sufficient capacity to force that decision on the elite, an intuition to which we will return. We refer to this latter, automatic transfer as *central implementation*. Many of our key results relate to the degree to which the implementation of reform is under local control, as captured by λ. Figure 2.1 provides a graphical illustration of this environment.

Following implementation of reform, the citizenry in each locality decides whether to rebel. We assume that the motivation to rebel is based entirely on expressive concerns, though, as we discuss, our results are robust to assuming that the citizenry values the contested resource directly. Peering behind the veil of a unitary citizenry, one can rationalize this assumption by assuming that the material gains from rebellion are non-excludable, whereas the "warm glow" from rebellion is experienced if and only if a citizen participates in rebellion.

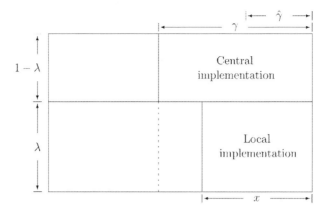

Figure 2.1 The policy environment. Proportion λ of an infinitely divisible resource is under control of the local elite, whereas proportion $1 - \lambda$ is under "central control." The elite chooses how much (x) of reform γ to locally implement; central control implies full implementation of γ. The status quo allocation under both local and central control is $\hat{\gamma}$.

In particular, we assume that the citizenry is more inclined to rebel, the larger its dissatisfaction with the implementation of reform. Formally, the citizenry compares the payoff from not rebelling, which we normalize to zero, to the expected payoff from rebelling, which we define as

$$\Gamma(x; \gamma) - \epsilon,$$

where $\Gamma(x; \gamma)$ denotes the citizenry's *grievance*, which is a function of the endogenous local implementation of reform x and the exogenous reform γ. The random variable ϵ represents the (material, psychological, etc.) cost of rebellion, drawn from distribution F, that is realized only after the elite chooses x. To keep the presentation tractable, we assume that F is the uniform distribution, with support $[-\sigma, \sigma]$, where σ is sufficiently large to ensure that, for any level of local implementation, the citizenry rebels with probability strictly between zero and one. This implies that the probability of rebellion, given local implementation x, is

$$\frac{\Gamma(x) + \sigma}{2\sigma}. \tag{2.1}$$

To capture the idea that reform is an incomplete contract against which subsequent implementation is measured, we assume that the citizenry's grievance is increasing in the degree to which local implementation x falls short of the promise of reform γ. (By assumption, central implementation is complete.) We also allow for the possibility that reform reduces the citizenry's grievance to the extent that the implementation of reform – central as well as

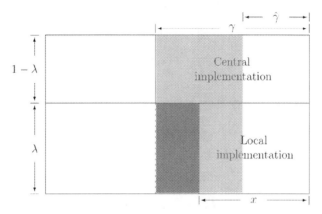

Figure 2.2 The citizenry's grievance is increasing in the degree to which local implementation x falls short of the promise of reform γ (area with dark shading) and decreasing in the degree to which the implementation of reform – central as well as local – improves on the status quo $\hat{\gamma}$ (area with light shading). The model parameterizes these two evaluations, with weight $1 - \beta$ given to the former and weight β given to the latter.

local – improves on the status quo $\hat{\gamma}$. Figure 2.2 illustrates these evaluations. We parameterize the relative importance of the two evaluations, such that weight $1 - \beta$ is given to the former and weight β given to the latter. Formally, the citizenry's grievance is

$$\Gamma\,(x;\gamma) = \overbrace{(1 - \beta)\,[\lambda(\gamma - x) + (1 - \lambda)(\gamma - \gamma)]}^{\text{Underimplementation}}$$

$$\underbrace{-\,\beta\,[\lambda\,(x - \hat{\gamma}) + (1 - \lambda)\,(\gamma - \hat{\gamma})]}_{\text{Gains over status quo}}.$$

Simplifying gives

$$\Gamma\,(x;\gamma) = \lambda\,(\gamma - x) - \beta\,(\gamma - \hat{\gamma})\,. \tag{2.2}$$

The citizenry's grievance is thus a weighted difference of the degree to which a) local implementation falls short of the promise of reform and b) the promise of reform improves on the status quo, where the weights on the two terms correspond to the degree of local implementation (λ) and the relative importance of the status quo in the citizenry's evaluation of gains and losses from reform (β).

Rebellion is costly to the elite. We assume that, in the event of a rebellion, the elite loses proportion $p \in (0, \gamma)$ of the resource under local control. (We can interpret the parameter p as the probability that the citizenry gains control of the local resource, which, for reasons already considered, does not enter the calculus to rebel; later we discuss robustness to relaxing this assumption. Alternatively, p may represent the destruction of some proportion of the local resource in the event of rebellion.) In contrast, if no rebellion is attempted, the elite transfers λx to the local citizenry. Finally, as previously assumed, regardless of whether the citizenry rebels, the elite transfers the exogenously mandated share $(1 - \lambda)\gamma$. The elite's preferences are represented by its expected share of the contested resource,

$$\Pr(\text{rebellion} \mid x)\,[\lambda\,(1 - p) + (1 - \lambda)(1 - \gamma)]$$
$$+ [1 - \Pr(\text{rebellion} \mid x)]\,[\lambda\,(1 - x) + (1 - \lambda)(1 - \gamma)].$$

Using Expression 2.1 and simplifying gives the equivalent expression

$$-x + \left[\frac{\Gamma(x) \mid \sigma}{2\sigma} \right] (x - p). \tag{2.3}$$

The elite chooses a level of local implementation x to maximize Expression 2.3. This is a concave problem, and the first-order condition is sufficient for a solution:

$$x^* = \max\left[\frac{1}{2}\left[p - \frac{1}{\lambda}[\sigma - (\lambda - \beta)\gamma - \beta\hat{\gamma}] \right], 0 \right].$$

At an interior solution (i.e., for $x^* > 0$), the elite provides a larger share of the locally controlled resource to the citizenry when the cost of rebellion p is large and when uncertainty about the citizenry's propensity to rebel σ is small. Of more interest is the effect of reform γ on local implementation x^*, which depends on the relationship between the parameters λ and β:

$$\frac{\partial x^*}{\partial \gamma}_{\mid x^* > 0} = \frac{1}{2} \cdot \frac{\lambda - \beta}{\lambda}. \tag{2.4}$$

When reform is predominantly locally implemented (i.e., when $\lambda > \beta$), implying that citizens' expressive motivations – and hence willingness to rebel – are driven by the degree to which local elites fail to deliver on the promise of reform, those elites unsurprisingly respond to an ambitious reform by surrendering more of the contested resource. In contrast, when reform is centrally implemented, citizens give credit for improvements on the status quo, regardless of whether those are actually fulfilled locally (see Equation 2.2); this reduces elites' incentive to implement reform.

Equation 2.4 illustrates a central fact about take-it-or-leave-it bargaining models with an outside option when the incentive to "rebel" (start a war, etc.) is driven by expressive rather than instrumental motivations: the grievances of the party with the outside option are incompletely internalized by the party that makes the offer. To see this, it is useful to compare our model to a "conventional" take-it-or-leave-it bargaining model with an outside option, where the party with that option is instrumentally motivated to obtain the contested resource. In such a model, a higher probability of successful rebellion has two effects – it increases the incentive to rebel, and it increases the cost of rebellion to the party making the offer. Under typical assumptions, these two effects cancel out (Fearon, 1995; Benson et al., 2016). In contrast, in a bargaining model where the incentive to rebel is driven by expressive motivations, a change in some parameter that affects grievances (here, γ) in general affects the incentive to rebel only.

Our central question is the relationship between reform and rebellion. Observe from Expression 2.1 and Equation 2.2 that this is

$$\frac{\partial \Pr(\text{rebellion} \mid x^*)}{\partial \gamma} = \frac{1}{2\sigma} \cdot \frac{\partial \Gamma(x^*)}{\partial \gamma}$$
$$= \frac{1}{2\sigma} \left[(\lambda - \beta) - \lambda \frac{\partial x^*}{\partial \gamma} \right].$$

The first term in the bracketed expression represents the direct effect of γ on rebellion, holding constant local implementation x^*, whereas the second term is the indirect effect through x^*, scaled by the degree to which reform is locally implemented. At a corner solution (i.e., for $x^* = 0$), this is equal to

$$\frac{\lambda - \beta}{2\sigma},$$

whereas at an interior solution, this is equal to

$$\frac{\lambda - \beta}{4\sigma},$$

given Equation 2.4. In either case, whether reform provokes or prevents rebellion depends on whether control over the implementation of reform is predominantly local ($\lambda > \beta$) or central ($\lambda < \beta$).

We can interpret this result as follows. Local implementation of reform drives a wedge between citizens' expectations of what reform promises and what actually happens. Elites may attempt to minimize this wedge, and thus the risk of rebellion, by carrying out some of what reform demands, but they discount the grievances arising from under-implementation. At the same time, the citizenry "gives credit" (where the parameter β measures the degree of credit) for reforms that improve on the status quo – this reduces grievances and the propensity to rebel. The former effect dominates the latter when reform is predominantly locally implemented.

We are now in a position to offer some preliminary answers to the questions raised in Section 1:

- *To what extent do the "certain groups" in a position to block implementation of reform internalize the resulting rebellion?* To a partial extent only. The expressive grievances in our model are only incompletely internalized by local elites.
- *Is there always a trade-off between stability and reform?* Yes. Any reform that incentivizes local implementation necessarily also increases the risk of rebellion. In Section 2.3 we explore whether there exists a trade-off between aggregate (local and central) implementation and stability.
- *Is reform indeed most dangerous for "bad governments"?* If by "bad government" we mean one with limited capacity to centrally implement reform, then yes. Reform is indeed most dangerous for such governments.

Our highly stylized model generates some sharp results. It is reasonable to ask whether these are driven by a number of simplifying assumptions. In Finkel and Gehlbach (2018), we consider various extensions and generalizations. We show that our qualitative results generalize to the case where the citizenry may be motivated to rebel not only for expressive reasons but also to seize control of the local resource, and we allow for the random cost of rebellion to be distributed much more generally.[9] We also demonstrate that the assumption of a unitary citizenry can be rationalized with a simple model of collective action among citizens of that locality. Finally, we demonstrate that the same qualitative results hold when we think of the elite and citizenry as local actors interacting with similar actors within a larger polity. In particular, if we assume (as in Passarelli and Tabellini, 2017) that the expressive benefit of rebellion is increasing in the number of localities that rebel, then the probability of rebellion is again increasing in reform if and only if $\lambda > \beta$.

2.3 Implications

As shown, whether reform provokes or prevents rebellion depends on whether local agents with a stake in the status quo are primarily responsible for its implementation. What determines whether this is the case? We see two possibilities, each of which we illustrate in the sections to follow.

First, when state capacity is relatively high, it may be possible to implement reform centrally. Capacious states are characterized by comparatively large bureaucracies (Schiavo-Campo et al., 1997; Gehlbach, 2008; Brown et al., 2009) organized around Weberian principles of meritocratic recruitment and internal promotion (Rauch and Evans, 2000). These features endow bureaucracies with the ability to implement reform as intended (Huber and McCarty,

---

[9] Formally, we assume that the distribution F is characterized by a strictly increasing hazard rate.

2004; Ting, 2011) and in a manner congruent with local conditions (Bendor and Meirowitz, 2004).[10] Absent this capacity, central governments may be forced to delegate authority to local agents with little interest in reform for its own sake. In some cases, the resulting "drift" from government intent can be minimized through the monitoring of these agents, which essentially amounts to central implementation, but weak states are often generally weak: the same limits to state capacity that necessitate local implementation may prevent the central government from holding local elites accountable.

Second, some reforms by their nature are easier than others to implement centrally. Universal rights can often be mandated from above, though even here monitoring may be necessary to ensure that those rights are enforced. Programs of redistribution, in contrast, may involve the reallocation of local property rights, which are often poorly understood by central authorities.

Our theory also has implications for the optimal choice of reform, though we do not model the selection of γ directly. Imagine a reformist but skittish central government interested in effecting the transfer of some contested resource from local elites to the citizenry but concerned about accompanying unrest. What is the optimal reform design?

On the one hand, regardless of the degree λ of local control over the implementation of reform, aggregate (local plus central) reform implementation is greater when reform is more ambitious.[11] To see this, observe that aggregate reform implementation is

$$R \equiv \lambda x^* + (1 - \lambda)\gamma,$$

where x^* is equilibrium local implementation. Differentiating with respect to γ gives

$$\frac{\partial R}{\partial \gamma} = \lambda \frac{\partial x^*}{\partial \gamma} + (1 - \lambda), \tag{2.5}$$

which is clearly positive if $x^* = 0$. Focus, then, on the case $x^* > 0$. Using Equation 2.4 gives

$$\frac{\partial R}{\partial \gamma}_{|x^*>0} = \frac{2 - \lambda - \beta}{2} > 0.$$

On the other hand, when the nature of reform or limits to state capacity necessitate local control over implementation (i.e., when $\lambda > \beta$), a more ambitious reform also implies more rebellion, as shown in Section 2.2. At some level, this

---

[10] For a review and further discussion, see Gailmard and Patty (2012).

[11] As with other results reported here, this holds under the more general case in which ϵ is drawn from generic distribution F with increasing hazard rate; see Finkel and Gehlbach (2018).

simply reflects the reality that in many environments the threat of rebellion is the only way to incentivize local elites to make concessions. Nonetheless, rebellion typically comes at a cost. When it does, the optimal reform design may set $\gamma < 1$, as the central government's interest in reform is balanced against its desire for stability.

2.4 Summary

Tocqueville's conjecture was that citizens ruled by "bad governments" would be most likely to rebel precisely when reform promised to change their lives for the better. In this section, we provide a microfoundation for this claim, showing that reforms that are introduced centrally but implemented locally create the conditions for rebellion by driving a wedge between what citizens expect and what they receive. By setting a reference point against which local implementation falls short, reform creates grievances that may be only partially offset by reform's improvement over the status quo. It is the failure of local elites to fully internalize these grievances that produces the "Tocqueville paradox."

Our theory suggests that the "bad governments" that Tocqueville describes will be those that lack capacity to implement reform centrally or to monitor local elites to ensure that reform is implemented as intended. In these circumstances, reform provokes rather than prevents rebellion. Conversely, when such capacity is present, reform reduces the risk of rebellion, allowing reformist governments to implement reform without risking social stability.

The same logic applies to the nature of reform itself. Weak states may be able to implement "simple" reforms centrally, even as strong states necessarily delegate complicated reforms to local agents. An implication of this perspective is that reformist governments may be more aggressive in pursuing the former type of reform, fearing the unrest that can follow the latter.

In the sections to follow, we explore the relationship between reform and rebellion in a number of important historical cases. In doing so, we ask: What was the capacity of the state and the nature of reform? How did these determine the degree of local control over reform? To what extent did local implementation "drift" from the promise of reform? And how did this affect the incidence of rebellion?

3 Russia

Two years before Abraham Lincoln issued his Emancipation Proclamation, Russian Tsar Alexander II declared the abolition of serfdom in most of the Russian Empire. The product of years of preparation, Alexander's emancipation was a momentous, far-reaching reform that touched nearly every part of

Russian society. As in America, Russian serfs obtained their legal freedom. In addition, and in sharp contrast to American emancipation, the process that unfolded in Russia included a vast program of land reform, whereby land rights and feudal obligations were renegotiated in anticipation of the eventual transfer of land from the nobility to the peasantry. Such a reform could only be carried out locally, with the participation of the nobility whose privileges were at stake. Much of the unrest that followed had its roots in that local implementation.

3.1 Historical Background

Compared to the rest of Europe, serfdom developed relatively late in Russia. Two factors – the government's decision to create a large class of military and civil servitors, and the land/labor ratio – led to its introduction (Domar, 1970). As Moscow's rulers embarked on a process of rapid territorial expansion, the large number of servitors needed for these activities were compensated by land grants (e.g., Kimerling Wirtschafter, 2008, p. 8). However, peasants' freedom of movement and the availability of yet-unsettled land put substantial economic pressure on the landed nobility. Restrictions on peasant mobility, introduced and enforced by the state, increased the attractiveness of state service. This process of gradual encroachment on peasants' freedom culminated during the late seventeenth and eighteenth centuries in the formal introduction of serfdom.

According to Russian legislation, serfs were bound to the land on which they lived, though de facto restrictions on mobility appear to have varied by region and estate (e.g., Dennison, 2011). They were required to provide the aristocratic landowners certain obligations, the most important of which were corvée (unpaid labor on landowner's fields, known in Russian as *barshchina*) and quitrent (payment in money or in kind, or *obrok*). Where the land was rich, such as in Ukraine's black-soil provinces, *barshchina* predominated; in the less fertile areas of northern Russia, where peasants tilled the land and were engaged in crafts and trade, *obrok* was prevalent. The combination of both was common. The landowner had policing and judicial powers over the serfs and was entitled to administer various punishments, such as flogging, imprisonment, and exile to Siberia. The serfs could also be sold, with or without land, at the landlord's whim (Zaionchkovskii, 1968).[12]

Not all peasants in the Russian Empire were serfs, however. By 1861, slightly less than half of Russia's peasants belonged to the state and appanage peasantry,

---

[12] In theory, existing legislation provided some protections, such as the landlord's obligation to ensure serfs' basic well-being, but these were minimally enforced.

who lived on state lands and lands owned by the royal family, respectively. The state peasantry, by far the larger of the two groups, was established in the early eighteenth century through the reforms of Peter the Great. Although initially subject to many of the same conditions as serfs, the Kiselev Reforms of 1837–1841 put state peasants under the control of the Ministry of State Properties and improved their economic and social status. Overall, state peasants tended to have larger land allotments than did serfs. Most important, unlike serfs, state peasants enjoyed greater rights to own property, engage in other occupations, and move to other social estates. The appanage peasants, in turn, were required to pay *obrok*, and like state peasants they had to pay taxes and fulfill several additional obligations, though their land allotments were generally smaller (Zaionchkovskii, 1968).

The original justification for serfdom was that serfs provided working hands and income for the nobles, who in turn were legally obliged to serve the tsar and the state. However, when this obligation ended in 1762, much of the moral justification for serfdom was lost. Furthermore, the often brutal and abusive treatment of serfs by the landlords or estate stewards, combined with the exploitation of peasants' labor, led to numerous instances of violence that ranged from killing or flogging landlords to massive peasant uprisings that devastated entire regions and required substantial military effort to quell. (The most notable of these, the Pugachev Rebellion during the reign of Catherine II, formed the basis of Pushkin's depiction of the "Russian revolt, senseless and merciless.")

By the early nineteenth century, serfdom was not only morally problematic but also simply dangerous to maintain. At the same time, the government was afraid to institute any drastic reforms. "Serfdom is a powder magazine under the state and the peasantry is an explosive mine," admitted Tsar Nicholas I (1825–1855), but "to tamper with it now would be, of course, an even more disastrous evil" (Volin, 1943, p. 48). Yet, some reforms did take place, mainly in the westernmost parts of the Empire. In 1816–1819, the serfs of the Baltic provinces (*gubernii*) in contemporary Estonia and Latvia were the first to be emancipated. However, while these peasants gained individual freedom, they received no land and therefore remained completely dependent on their former lords as hired laborers. In 1837, as discussed, the government initiated a major reform substantially improving the status of state peasants. Finally, in the late 1840s, an "inventory reform," regulating peasants' land allotments and obligations, was introduced in the right-bank Ukraine, with a clear goal of limiting the powers of the largely Polish Catholic nobility. Abuses of this process by the gentry provoked widespread peasant disturbances that prefigure the events that we will describe (Moon, 2001b).

The main catalyst for reform was Russia's defeat in the Crimean War (1853–1856), which clearly demonstrated its outdated institutions.[13] The war also led to numerous instances of unrest because of increased conscription of peasants to the military and attempted migration (fueled by false rumors of freedom for serfs upon joining the wartime militia) or settlement in Crimea in the aftermath of the fighting (Zaionchkovskii, 1968, pp. 64–65). While serfdom was profitable for landowners (Domar and Machina, 1984),[14] the central government's increasing fear of peasant rebellion (Gerschenkron, 1965) and general understanding that major institutional change was necessary made emancipation unavoidable. On December 4, 1858, Alexander publicly announced that serfdom was soon to be abolished.

3.2 Emancipation

3.2.1 Reform Design

As the nobility internalized the general idea of emancipation, however reluctantly, a decisive battle was waged over the reform's content. Standard historical accounts present the reform drafting process as a bitter struggle between *krepostniki* (supporters of serfdom) and liberals, with the two groups divided on whether emancipation should be accompanied by the distribution of land to former serfs. In fact, the divisions ran deeper, involving cleavages between Westernizers and Slavophiles, as well as between those who viewed the peasants through the prism of romanticism and those who adopted a more rationalist, individualist view of the peasant (Khristoforov, 2011, p. 9).[15] Navigating between these camps, Alexander rejected the idea of landless emancipation, but at the same time he could not order the radical reform envisaged by the liberal bureaucracy. The ultimate design was a complicated and convoluted compromise that fell short of each camp's desires.

The reform went into effect on February 19, 1861. Serfs were granted immediate personal freedom and the right to own personal property, including the

---

[13] Dennison (2011) demonstrates that Russian serfdom was far more variegated than conventionally assumed, with some estates providing a legal and administrative framework that fostered rural economic development. Nonetheless, various constraints prevented such institutions from being universally adopted.

[14] Though likely inefficient: see Markevich and Zhuravskaya (2018).

[15] Related to and in parallel with these debates, the government began planning to reform government institutions and state–society relations at the local level. Naturally, these discussions were heavily influenced by Tocqueville's *The Ancien Régime and the Revolution*, which was published the year the Crimean War ended and was widely read by Russian elites. Although influential with respect to the question of government centralization and local institutions, Tocqueville's analysis was overlooked by Russian readers when it came to reform's potential danger (Starr, 2015, pp. 71–90).

right to "redeem" (buy out) their houses and adjacent garden plots. The reform also introduced minimum and maximum personal allotments of arable land, which varied with soil type. The landowner and peasants had the option to agree on an immediate "grant allotment" of one-quarter of the maximum allotment, for which the peasant would not be required to pay or provide obligations. If peasants wished instead to receive their full land allotment, they became "temporarily obligated" until such time as the landowner chose to begin the "redemption" operation that transferred ownership to the peasantry. The terms of temporary obligation – and, typically, the subsequent redemption process – were then established during a two-year transition period, as regulatory charters (*ustavnye gramoty*) specifying land allotments, payments, and the general framework of landlord–peasant relations were compiled by the landlord in cooperation with the peasantry. Transactions were not between the landlord and individual peasants but between the landlord and the entire local peasant community, the *sel'skoe obshchestvo*, which was subsequently held collectively responsible for the redemption payments of its members; former serfs could not leave the commune unless they paid off their full share of the community obligation.[16]

3.2.2 State Capacity and Local Implementation

A key feature of Russian emancipation was the inability of the central government to carry out reform on its own. Outside of major urban centers, the Russian state's control of its territory was limited at best. As Skocpol (1979) notes, "[i]mperial jurisdiction stopped just outside the doors of the noble-owned serf estates" (p. 89), which is precisely where the government needed to be to implement the reform. The state's weakness was an inevitable outcome of the monarchy's conscious policy of reliance on the nobility as its local agents. Ironically, the peasant revolts of the seventeenth and eighteenth centuries had "convince[d] the state of the value of the nobility as a police force in the provinces" (Moon, 2001a, p. 27).

The government's weakness extended to the very center of the state apparatus. The Russian government did not have the expertise, the institutional capacity, or the coercive power to carry out reform on its own. It didn't even know the lay of the land. Although the central government conducted a number of cadastral surveys prior to emancipation, no national cadastre existed at the time of reform (Evtuhov, 2011). Land surveyors were in short supply and

---

[16] Plans to subsidize redemption payments were shelved after the banking crisis in 1859, thus increasing the expected flow of payments by serfs who gained ownership of their land (Hoch, 1991).

of uncertain professional ability (Khristoforov, 2011; Castañeda Dower and Markevich, 2017). Local police forces were so small, neglected, and underpaid (indeed, in some cases unpaid) that "the head of the national force questioned whether Russia in fact had a police system" (Starr, 2015, pp. 46, 116). To the extent that local police did exist, they were often preoccupied with such tasks as firefighting and supervision of philanthropic work (Starr, 2015, p. 143) and in any case were largely under the control of the local elites that stood to lose from reform. The only way to carry out such an ambitious reform was to delegate its implementation to local actors with a stake in the pre-existing status quo – that is, to the nobility themselves.

Reform's local implementation became its key challenge. In principle, the peasants were entitled to their existing land allotments, but so ambitious a reform and the very fact that the reform's content was a compromise among numerous conflicting policy proposals provided local elites with ample opportunities for gerrymandering – mainly in cases where the existing allotment was below the stipulated minimum or, as was often the case, exceeded the envisaged maximum (in which case existing allotments were "cut off"). Numerous landlords jumped at the opportunity to keep the estate's best land for themselves and to ensure that former serfs received as little valuable land as possible.

Anticipating potential conflicts between dissatisfied peasants and landowners, as part of the emancipation reform the government created the new institution of "peace arbitrators" (*mirovye posredniki*), tasked with the verification of charters and the resolution of conflicts between landlords and the newly liberated peasants.[17] Nonetheless, even for this institution the weak Russian state was forced to rely on local elites. Regional governors were asked to find reform sympathizers from among the local landowning (and often serfowning) nobility to fill these positions; Leo Tolstoy was a notable example (Ust'iantseva, 1992; Easley, 2002). In some areas, however, supporters of emancipation among the nobility were nowhere to be found, and, government efforts notwithstanding, individuals of "every political stripe, with varying degrees of vulnerability to local pressures" were drafted into the institution (Easley, 2002, p. 711). Many found it hard to be neutral while the interests of neighboring landlords were at stake, and some used outright violence, including flogging, to compel peasants to accept the charter terms.

---

[17] A landowner was given a year to draw up the charter, with or without consultation with the peasants. After that period, the arbitrator could draft the charter independently. Although initially both sides had to approve the charter terms, eventually a refusal to sign ceased to be an obstacle to implementation. Indeed, of the 73,195 charters in effect at the start of 1863, approximately half had not been signed by the peasants (Easley, 2002, pp. 721–726).

Even when the arbitrators were willing to confront local elites, the landlords were often able to neutralize the "troublesome" mediators by using a combination of political, psychological, and even physical pressure. "They want to beat me up, they want me to be put on trial . . . I am simply waiting until they calm down a bit (*pougomonilis'*) and then I will retire," wrote Tolstoy about his relations with local landlords (Ust'iantseva, 1992, p. 179). Tolstoy's experience is far from unique: from 1861 to 1863, more than 25 percent of arbitrators quit their roles, often as a result of pressure and hostility from landowners (Easley, 2002, p. 727). With peace arbitrators sidelined and with no accountability to the central government, the implementation of reform became a purely local process.

3.3 Reform and Rebellion

3.3.1 Data

What was the impact of emancipation on peasant unrest? To answer this question, we turn to data we compiled with Tricia Olsen on various disturbances between 1851 and 1871 (Finkel, Gehlbach, and Olsen, 2015), using four volumes of *Krest'ianskoe Dvizhenie v Rossii* (*The Peasant Movement in Russia*), a chronicle of peasant actions between 1796 and 1917 (Okun', 1962; Okun' and Sivkov, 1963; Ivanov, 1964; Zaionchkovskii and Paina, 1968). The events in these volumes were gathered by a team of Soviet historians, working during the Khrushchev Thaw, based on two main sources of information. The first of these is the archival collections of the main Soviet archives – the Central State Historical Archive of the USSR (TsGIA), the Central State Archive of the October Revolution (TsGAOR), and the Central State Military-Historical Archive (TsGVIA) – and several smaller archives. These archives (and their successors) house, among other materials, the documents of the Imperial Court; the State Council; the political police (Third Section); the Ministries of Internal Affairs, Justice, and State Properties; the Senate; and the highest governing body of the Russian Orthodox Church. They also include reports to central authorities by provincial governors, state officials, and police officers; final reports of various inspections; archives of large landholding families; and similar documents. The second main source used to compile the chronicle is numerous secondary historical works on peasant unrest, emancipation, and rural life in various provinces.

We coded all entries from 1851 to 1871 – that is, the decade before and after emancipation. Doing so generates a dataset of 3,775 events across 55 provinces which today constitute the Baltic States; Belarus; Moldova; most of Ukraine, Armenia, and Georgia; and almost all of European Russia. Of these events,

Ранее 29 июня — 6 июля. Симбирская губ. Отказ вр.-об. крестьян деревень Каирова, Недремаловки, Протопоповки, Перетяжкиной и с. Шатра-шаны Буинского у. в имениях Сабаниных, Горемыкина, Пятницкого и Чертковой запахивать свои паровые поля из-за отрезки хорошей земли; была введена военная команда.
  ЦГИА, ф. 1291, оп. 52, 1862 г., д. 117, л. 1—6, 13—16; ЦГАОР, ф. 109-И, 4 эксп., 1862 г., д. 223, л. 21—27; ЦГВИА, ф. 395, оп. 299, ОА, 1862 г., д. 362, л. 49—50, 101—101 об., 108—109 об., 117—117 об.; *Левашев*, стр. 54.

Figure 3.1 A typical chronicle entry from *Krest'ianskoe Dvizhenie v Rossii* (*The Peasant Movement in Russia*), indicating that in June and July, 1862, peasants in several villages on several estates refused to plow their fallow fields in response to a "cutoff" of good land. Troops were called out in response to the unrest. The indented text at the bottom gives the archival sources on which the entry is based.

277 involve state and/or appanage peasants only. Most of the remaining entries explicitly mention the involvement of current or former serfs, alone or (rarely) in combination with state and/or appanage peasants. For 134 entries, there is no mention of peasant type. We assume for such events the involvement of (for-mer) serfs, given the preponderance of such events in the data, but the statistical results we report are robust to dropping such events from the sample.

The information in the chronicles is quite rich, allowing us to characterize events using categories similar to those in other analyses of event data (e.g., Robertson, 2011). Figure 3.1 depicts a typical entry. For each event, we are able to identify one or more actions taken by peasants at a particular time and place. For more than half the events, the chronicle also provides the proxi-mate cause of the action, as identified by various observers. Many events also indicate some sort of response by local officials (typically the arrival of a mil-itary detachment). With the assistance of a native-Russian research assistant, we developed a coding protocol based on analysis of a subsample of events from various years. We then manually coded all events during the sample window: first by our research assistant and then again by one of us (a native Russian speaker), with discrepancies resolved in favor of the latter's judgment in consultation with the other authors.

In what follows, we drop events in Estliand, Kurliand, and Lifliand (contemporary Estonia and Latvia), where emancipation took place decades earlier. In addition, we drop events in Bessarabiia, Dagestan, Erivan, Kutaisi, and Tiflis – five outlying provinces where emancipation was implemented later. The final sample is 3,629 events in 47 provinces.[18] Of these, we are able to

---

[18] Unlike in Finkel, Gehlbach, and Olsen (2015), where the analysis is province-level, we do not recode events in Ufa as belonging to Orenburg. Further, we do not drop events in Stavropol, as

further establish the district (*uezd*) in which the event took place for 3,353 events, or over 90 percent of the sample. The narrative discussion and figures (with the exception of Figure 3.6) in the following section use the full sample; the statistical analysis in the appendix uses the subsample for which district is identified.

3.3.2 Dynamics of Unrest

To understand the impact of the Emancipation Reform on peasant unrest, it is essential to know what unrest looked like *before* emancipation. It is also helpful to compare unrest among (former) serfs, who were directly affected by the Emancipation Reform of 1861, with that among state and appanage peasants, who were not. Figure 3.2 illustrates yearly dynamics among both groups of peasants for two major classes of events in our data: a) *refusals* to pay *obrok* (quitrent), provide *barshchina* (corvée), and more generally to provide various obligations; and b) various acts of *theft and violence*, including against the landowner and estate management.[19] For both groups of peasants, there are relatively few reported disturbances during the early and mid-1850s and mid- to late 1860s. The uptick in serf unrest in 1858 (persisting for theft and violence through 1859) seems to reflect an increase in disturbances in the wake of the Crimean War, which, as discussed, was part of the context in which plans for emancipation were made. During the early 1860s, however, there is a marked increase among former serfs in incidence of refusals and theft/violence. Notably, there is no analogous increase among state and appanage peasants.

Figure 3.2 is strongly suggestive of a causal effect of reform on rebellion, but it is impossible to make strong claims solely from graphical presentation of the raw data. In the appendix to this section, we present results from a differences-in-differences research design, in which we compare the district-level incidence of unrest among (former) serfs to that among state and appanage peasants during three periods: 1851 to 1860 (the pre-emancipation period), 1861 and 1862 (the "transition period" during which the terms of emancipation were worked

---

we do not require the missing population data for that province for the fixed-effects regressions reported in the appendix.

[19] We define refusals more narrowly than in Finkel, Gehlbach, and Olsen (2015) to include only those events that are obviously disruptive to estate management. The following actions are classified as theft and violence: seizure of landowner's property (general), seizure of landowner's property (forest/lumber), seizure of public property, (attempted) destruction of landowner's property, (attempted) destruction of public property, (attempted) destruction of pub, violence against landlord/family, violence against landlord/family (murder), violence against management (general), violence against management (murder), violence against public authority, prisoners freed, and unspecified unrest (typically rendered as *volnenie*).

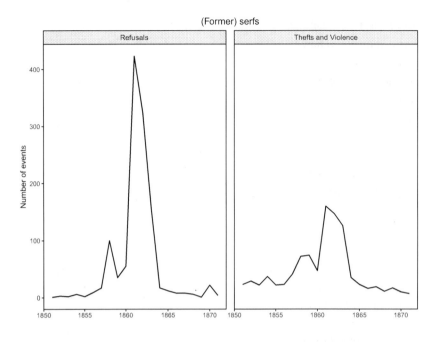

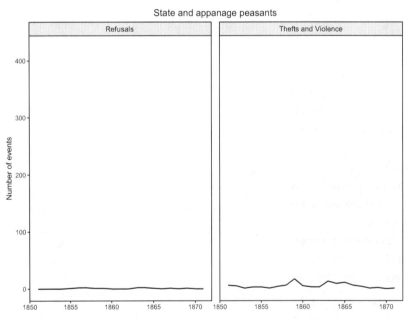

Figure 3.2 Annual number of events involving refusals and theft and violence, respectively, for (former) serfs (top panel) and state and appanage peasants (bottom panel), 1851 to 1871.

out on individual estates), and 1863 to 1871 (the post-emancipation period).[20] Our empirical strategy controls for time-invariant district characteristics that may differentially affect unrest among the two groups of peasants (including most obviously the district-level population of each peasant group). We also consider various potential sources of measurement error and other confounders, including heightened monitoring of peasant unrest by the Ministry of Internal Affairs during the years just before and after the announcement of reform, the possibility that unrest among former serfs was more likely to have entered the archives due to the presence of "peace arbitrators" during the transition period, and weather shocks. We also take into account various forms of spatial correlation and consider alternative strategies to account for the presence of "irrelevant" events in our data. Regardless of measurement or specification, the general pattern is very clear: there is a large increase in both refusals and theft/violence among (former) serfs during the transition period that is not reflected among state and appanage peasants, followed by a reversion to pre-emancipation levels of unrest during the post-emancipation period. For our baseline specification, this amounts to a relative increase during the transition period of approximately 0.85 refusals (a roughly 1,800-percent increase), and 0.30 acts of theft and violence (a 400-percent increase), per district-year among (former) serfs.

Why did unrest among former serfs increase so markedly after emancipation? One possibility can be quickly discarded – that reform made it easier for such peasants to rebel. Although serfs were granted legal freedom in 1861, the tsar and his bureaucrats were careful not to provide greater opportunity for social unrest. Restrictions on peasant mobility were retained after emancipation, out of fear that a more mobile population would be more volatile (Moon, 2001a, p. 126). Moreover, there was no sharp discontinuity in the state's capacity for repression. The nobility retained their grip over the local police and, as we will discuss, it was military action that helped to bring the disturbances to an end.

In principle, former serfs may have nonetheless interpreted emancipation as a signal of the central state's weakness, in response to which they chose to rebel. In practice, peasants rebelled "in the name of the tsar" (Field, 1976),

---

[20] Formally, the transition period ran from February 19, 1861, through February 18, 1863, though the Emancipation Manifesto and Statutes were published on March 5, 1861 (Moon, 2001a, pp. 71–72, 84). We define the transition period in annual terms to incorporate events for which "season" (e.g., winter, start of year) but not month is identified in the chronicle entry. As illustrated, there are comparatively few events recorded in January of either year, though there is a (last) spike in February 1863.

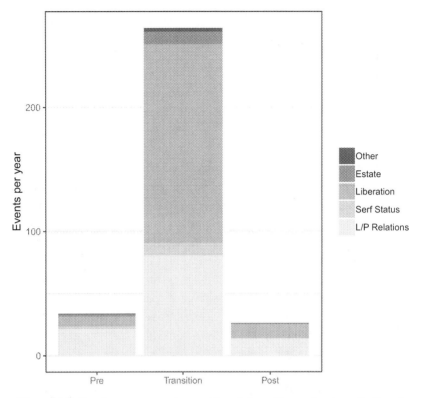

Figure 3.3 Proximate cause of unrest involving either refusals or theft and violence for (former) serfs. "L/P" = landlord/peasant. Transition period is 1861 and 1862.

not against him. The actions we will describe were overwhelmingly directed toward local elites.

Rather than changes in the cost of collective action or perceptions of state capacity, unrest among former serfs seems to be driven by grievances related to the very terms and process of emancipation. Figure 3.3 provides the proximate cause, where noted, of refusals and theft/violence among such peasants during the three periods that we examine. Using the categories established in Finkel, Gehlbach, and Olsen (2015), we distinguish among events driven by a) *landlord/peasant relations*, including the provision of various obligations, brutal treatment, and the forced enlistment of serfs in the military; b) *serf status*, including desire to be released from such status or transferred to the state peasantry; c) *liberation*, incorporating rumors of liberation, anticipation of a "second liberation," dissatisfaction with the terms of emancipation, and distribution of printed materials calling for peasants to liberate themselves; d) dissatisfaction with *estate* management or municipal government;

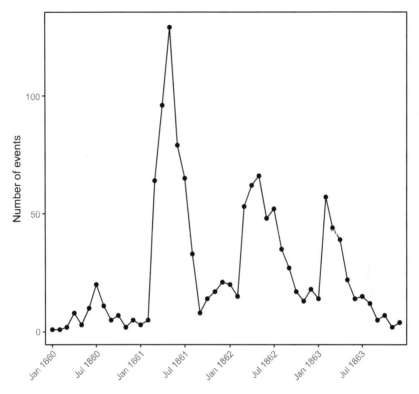

Figure 3.4 Monthly number of events involving either refusals or theft and violence for (former) serfs, 1860 to 1863.

and e) *other* causes. The largest increase during the transition period is in events concerning liberation. Of these, the overwhelming majority are driven by dissatisfaction with the terms of liberation.

Behind this generalized grievance with the terms of emancipation lie at least two distinct phenomena, corresponding to different phases in the evolution of unrest during the transition period. As Figure 3.4 illustrates, there was a sharp spike in unrest among former serfs in the spring of 1861, which is when the Emancipation Manifesto was read out in village churches across European Russia (Moon, 2001a, p. 89). The Manifesto itself was poorly worded, leading the writer Ivan Turgenev to declare that it "was evidently written in French and translated into clumsy Russian by some German" (Moon, 2001a, p. 83),[21] and many peasants apparently understood (incorrectly) that they had been

---

[21] French was the preferred language of communication of the Russian elite. Germans from the Baltic provinces played an important role in the Empire's administration.

completely liberated of any obligations to the estate owner.[22] Even when the Manifesto was understood, some peasants doubted its authenticity, believing that estate owners had substituted a watered-down document for the "real" emancipation. Confusion and exaggerated expectations (elements outside of the theory presented earlier) provoked numerous acts of defiance, some of which were quite large. In spring 1861, for example, approximately nine thousand peasants in Saratov refused to cultivate their landlords' fields and began preparations for an armed uprising; military units were called in to put down the unrest. In Chernigov, more than 26,000 peasants protested against their landlords, and troops sent to quell the unrest were attacked by armed villagers. More than 80,000 peasants were involved in various disturbances in Podolia, which ultimately were put down by the military.[23]

Most of the ambiguity about the nature and design of emancipation was apparently resolved when the peace arbitrators arrived that summer (Pushkarev, 1968; Moon, 2001a, p. 94). It was at this point that the process of drafting regulatory charters began in earnest. A second wave of unrest began in the spring of 1862 (see Figure 3.4), but this time disturbances were substantially driven by rejections of the land allotments and obligations laid down in regulatory charters. Figure 3.5 illustrates the dynamics of unrest involving such rejections: sharply increasing in March 1862, a steady decline through the remainder of the year, and then another spike in early 1863 as the deadline for completing the regulatory charters approached and passed.[24]

Figure 3.1 is representative of events during this second phase of unrest. Encouraged by peace arbitrators to understand emancipation in the limited terms intended by the tsar and his bureaucrats, peasants were nonetheless disappointed by the actual settlements imposed on them by local landowners, who abused their control of the process to cut off peasants' existing land allotments, provide them with different allotments, resettle peasants to different land entirely, and more generally ensure that the estate's most fertile lands would remain in the landlord's hands. The consequences of these decisions were far-reaching, extending beyond the period of temporary obligation to communal ownership of arable land through the redemption process. The grievances that emerged from this process of drafting regulatory charters

---

[22] Chronicle entries from this period tend to have a certain structure: peasant actions are driven by former serfs' "interpretation of the manifesto in the spirit of peasant demands" (*tolkovanie manifesta v dukhe krest'ianskikh trebovanii*).

[23] Okun' and Sivkov (1963), pp. 686 (Saratov), 695 (Chernigov), and 714 (Podolia).

[24] As with the other analysis in this section, Figure 3.5 restricts attention to events that (also) involve refusals and theft/violence, as defined earlier. The pattern is similar, though the swings are of larger magnitude, if one allows for any rejection of the terms of emancipation, regardless of whether such events meet our (narrow) definition of refusal or involve theft/violence.

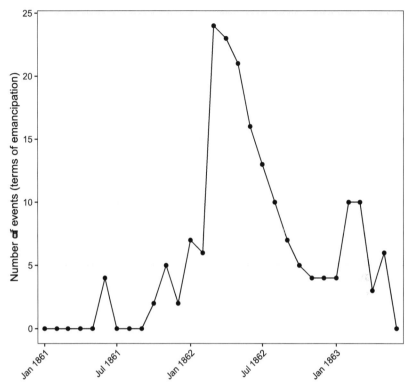

Figure 3.5 Monthly number of events involving either refusals or theft and violence, January 1861 to July 1863, in which peasants rejected terms of emancipation.

encouraged former serfs to act, or refuse to act, in myriad ways harmful to landowners' interests. The landowners must have anticipated this response and indeed may have made some concessions to reduce its severity, but, consistent with our theoretical framework, they nonetheless pushed ahead in a manner that furthered their own interests while stoking peasants' sense of injury.

Such grievances were most pronounced in the *chernozem*, or "black soil" region. Figure 3.6 illustrates the correlation: a sharp band of unrest involving rejections of terms of emancipation in the southern districts where soil was most fertile.[25] (In Table 3.3 in the appendix, we show that this correlation

---

[25] We use GIS-coded data on soil type from the Food and Agriculture Organization (FAO), available at www.fao.org/nr/land/soils/harmonized-world-soil-database/download-data-only/jp/, which we overlay on a map of nineteenth-century Russian administrative boundaries. The resulting dataset provides the proportion of land in each district belonging to one of twenty-two soil types or to other categories such as water. Based on a classification by Brady and Weil (2002), we define *fertile soil* as any of the following soil types observed in our data: Chernozem, Greyzem, Histosol, Kastanozem, Phaeozem, or Vertisol.

Fertile soil

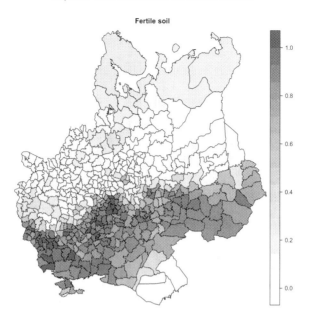

Unrest involving refusal to accept terms of liberation

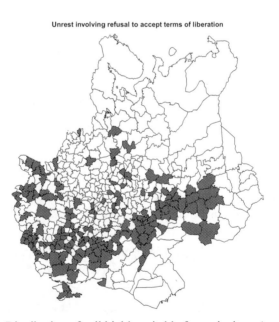

Figure 3.6 Distribution of soil highly suitable for agriculture (top panel) and presence of events involving either refusals or theft and violence, 1861 and 1862, in which peasants rejected terms of emancipation (bottom panel).

is generally robust to conditioning on the size of the former serf population [more serfs imply greater opportunity for unrest], to defining the outcome as a dummy variable or a count, to conditioning on province fixed effects, and to various methods of correcting for spatial correlation in unobserved determinants of unrest.) Most obviously, in regions with highly fertile soil, landowners were incentivized to seize as much good land as possible, but other factors may have also played a role. On the one hand, *barshchina* was more prevalent in the *chernozem*. In such districts the peasant commune played an important role in organizing work on the demesne (Hoch, 1989), plausibly creating capacity for collective action. On the other, where peasants lived in comparatively large settlements, as was more common in black-soil districts, the benefits of collective action would have been concentrated among a relatively large group. By the logic of collective action (Olson, 1965), it would have been more difficult to encourage participation in unrest in such environments. Unfortunately, absent strong assumptions, there is no straightforward way to sort out these various effects, as peasant organization is a consequence of – and thus "post-treatment" relative to – soil fertility (Rosenbaum, 1984).

By the summer of 1863, peasant unrest had receded. It remained low for the remainder of the decade (Figure 3.2). What explains this sharp decline? One possibility, suggested by Passarelli and Tabellini's (2017) model of emotions and political unrest, is that the reference points against which any gains or losses were measured shifted after the regulatory charters were completed and peace arbitrators went home. With little chance that the charters would be modified, former serfs became resigned to what they received through the emancipation settlements. Such an interpretation is broadly consistent with the timing of the drop-off in unrest, though it should be emphasized that the redemption process stretched on for years after the transition period.

Two other developments may have helped to keep things quiet. First, the repressive capacity mobilized during the unrest – in addition to numerous police and internal security forces, more than eighty infantry and cavalry regiments were involved in quelling peasant disturbances in various parts of the Russian Empire (Zaionchkovskii, 1968, pp. 166–167) – remained active for some time after completion of the regulatory charters. As shown in Figure 3.7, the proportion of events involving some sort of military response was high through the mid-1860s. Second, in 1864 a new institution of local self-government was created: the *zemstvo*. Although representation in the district *zemstvo* assemblies was heavily skewed toward the nobility – indeed, more so where there was a history of peasant unrest (Castañeda Dower et al., 2018) – the opportunity to influence policy through representative institutions may have reduced the incentive to rebel.

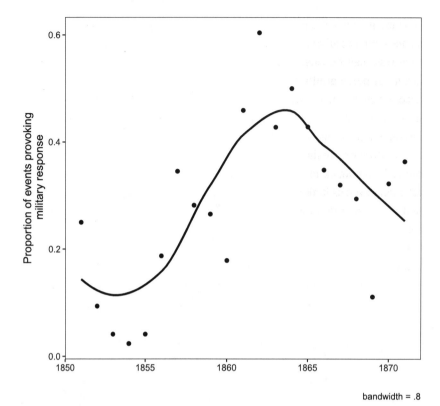

bandwidth = .8

Figure 3.7 Proportion of events provoking military response among those
involving either refusals or theft and violence for (former) serfs, 1851 to 1871.

3.4 Conclusion

In concluding the previous section, we posed four questions to guide our analysis of historical cases: What was the capacity of the state and the nature of
reform? How did these determine the degree of local control over reform?
To what extent did local implementation "drift" from the promise of reform?
And how did this affect the incidence of rebellion? For the case of Russian
emancipation, we can answer these questions as follows.

   At the time of emancipation, the Russian state had little presence in the countryside, which is where the extensive land reform envisioned by Alexander and
his bureaucrats was to take place.

   As a consequence, much of the actual administration of reform was delegated to local landowners, whose biases were only partially compensated by
the arrival of "peace arbitrators" named by the government.

   Unsurprisingly, the local nobility exploited their control over reform to
gerrymander land allotments in their favor, stoking grievances among former
serfs who expected more from reform.

These grievances encouraged numerous acts of violent and nonviolent resistance – but not all of the unrest that followed publication of the Emancipation Manifesto can be closely tied to local implementation. It took time and the arrival of peace arbitrators for peasants' expectations of what reform should accomplish to settle. Before they did, and even before the process of local implementation had begun, peasants were encouraged to rebel by confused interpretations of the nature of reform.

The story of Russian emancipation thus illustrates the potential of our theoretical framework to explain the empirical relationship between reform and rebellion, even as it highlights a key assumption of our model – that the extent and nature of reform are common knowledge. In the discussion to follow, we again pose these four questions, using theory to inform our understanding of historical cases, even as we use those cases to examine the limits of our theory.

3.5 Appendix: Econometric Evidence

3.5.1 Panel Regressions

To plausibly identify an effect of emancipation on unrest, we employ a difference-in-differences research design that exploits a key feature of Russian emancipation: the Emancipation Reform of 1861 had a direct effect only on serfs, not on state or appanage peasants. Our data allow us to separately estimate the rate of disturbances for these two groups of peasants at different points in time, from which we can compare the change over time in the rate for each group.

We estimate linear models with district fixed effects.[26] For each group of peasants, we estimate

$$d_{it} = \mathbf{w}_t \beta + \alpha_i + \epsilon_{it}, \tag{3.1}$$

where d_{it} is the count of disturbances (refusals or theft/violence) in district i in year t; $\mathbf{w}_t$ is a vector of time variables, with associated parameter vector β; α_i is a district fixed effect; and ϵ_{it} is an idiosyncratic error term.[27] We assume $\mathbf{w}_t = (x_t, y_t)$, where x_t is a dummy variable equal to one if $t = 1861$ or $t = 1862$ and zero otherwise, and y_t is a dummy variable equal to one if $t > 1862$ and zero otherwise. Thus, we estimate the change in the rate of peasant disturbances for the two-year transition period and the post-emancipation period, relative to

---

[26] As is typical when count outcomes are all small in magnitude, the estimated marginal effects from the linear models reported here are remarkably similar to those from Poisson models (with fixed effects).

[27] As the number of peasants in some group is relatively time-invariant (and in any event not measured annually), the fixed effects implicitly pick up the district-level population for that group.

the pre-emancipation baseline. Our difference-in-differences estimates come from comparing the estimates of β for landowner and non-landowner peasants, respectively. With one exception, as we will discuss, we report standard errors corrected to allow for correlation of error terms within fifty provinces.

Table 3.1 presents results for various specifications and samples for peasant disturbances involving refusals. Column 1 is our baseline specification. We run separate models for (former) serfs and state/appanage peasants, estimating in each case the rate of disturbances during the pre-emancipation, transition, and post-emancipation periods. The results indicate a precisely estimated increase of approximately 0.85 events per district-year in refusals among (former) serfs during the transition period versus a tiny, statistically insignificant decrease among state and appanage peasants: the difference-in-differences estimate is thus very close to the estimate for (former) serfs alone. For both groups of peasants, the rate of disturbances during the post-emancipation period is very similar to that in the pre-emancipation period.

One potential concern with these results is that the process by which disturbances entered the chronicles on which our data are based might have differed for (former) serfs and state/appanage peasants. In general, there is little reason to suspect disproportionately high reporting of disturbances involving (former) serfs: disturbances among state peasants would likely have entered the archives more easily, given reporting requirements for stewards on state lands and, as discussed, the chroniclers themselves emphasized that they were focused on emerging class consciousness among the peasantry as a whole. To the extent that disturbances are less frequent among state peasants – though they are also infrequent among (former) serfs at the beginning and end of our sample window – this may reflect the generally larger land allotments and lower dues for peasants on state lands (e.g., Hoch, 2004, p. 249). That said, it is possible that events involving former serfs would have been better documented during the transition period due to the presence of the peace arbitrators. To check for this possibility, we restrict attention to events drawn from the archive TsGAOR, which are primarily disturbances recorded by the tsarist political police, which was active throughout the period we examine. Column 2 shows that our qualitative results are robust to this change in measurement, with the smaller difference-in-differences estimate reflecting the smaller number of events meeting this criterion.[28]

---

[28] There are approximately 0.13 refusals involving (former) serfs per district-year for the baseline measure versus 0.05 refusals per district-year when restricting attention to events drawn from TsGAOR. For state/appanage peasants, there are no events exclusively drawn from TsGAOR during the transition period.

Table 3.1 Peasant Unrest: Refusals

	Binary (1)	TsGAOR only (2)	1858–1862 (3)	Large events (4)	Binary outcome (5)	Spatial errors (6)	Drop western (7)	Weather shocks (8)
			(Former) serfs					
Transition period	0.848 (0.073)	0.399 (0.047)	0.765 (0.072)	0.384 (0.040)	0.433 (0.027)	0.817 (0.026)	0.796 (0.077)	0.853 (0.081)
Post-emancipation period	0.004 (0.010)	0.009 (0.003)		0.009 (0.005)	0.006 (0.007)	0.000 (0.016)	0.001 (0.011)	0.011 (0.012)
Provincial rye price								−0.053 (0.040)
			State and appanage peasants					
Transition period	−0.001 (0.001)	−0.000 (0.000)	−0.001 (0.001)	−0.000 (0.000)	−0.001 (0.001)	−0.001 (0.001)	−0.001 (0.001)	−0.001 (0.001)
Post-emancipation period	0.000 (0.001)	0.001 (0.000)		0.001 (0.001)	0.000 (0.001)	0.000 (0.001)	0.001 (0.001)	0.001 (0.001)
Provincial rye prices								0.001 (0.004)
Observations	9,849	9,849	2,345	9,849	9,849	9,849	7,959	7,529
District FEs	Yes	Yes	Yes	Yes	Yes	Yes	Yes	Yes

Notes: Linear fixed-effects models on a panel of districts in European Russia from 1851 to 1871. The outcome is number of refusals (see text for definition), but for Model 5, where the outcome is presence of at least one such event. Models for (former) serfs and state/appanage peasants run separately. Transitition period is 1861 and 1862. Model 2 restricts the analysis to events drawn from the archive TsGAOR, whereas Model 3 restricts the sample to the years 1858–1862. Model 4 considers only disturbances involving more than one village or district. Model 6 is a spatial panel fixed-effects model, implemented using the sp1m package in R, that models spatial autoregressive errors with an inverse-distance weighting matrix. Model 7 drops districts in nine western provinces. In parentheses, standard errors that correct for clustering at the provincial level (but for Model 6).

A related concern is the increased frequency from 1858 through 1862 with which the Ministry of Internal Affairs provided reports on peasant affairs to the tsar. That said, documents of the Ministry of Internal Affairs were primarily culled from the archive TsGIA for the chronicles on which our data are based, so the restriction to events in TsGAOR already corrects for the possibility that events entered the dataset more readily during this period. As an additional check, we restrict the sample to the years 1858–1862 and estimate the change in number of refusals during the transition period, relative to the previous three years. Column 3 shows that the difference-in-differences estimate is similar in magnitude to that in Column 1.

In the preceding analysis, the district-year count of disturbances is based on discrete entries in the chronicles on which our data are based, regardless of the events' magnitude. In practice, peasant disturbances vary greatly in scale. In addition, there is some inconsistency in the chronicles in whether multiple events are aggregated up to a single entry. Unfortunately, we have a precise estimate of the number of peasants involved only for a small fraction of events in our sample, so we employ two alternative strategies to check that our results are not driven by such considerations. First, we restrict attention to disturbances affecting more than one village or district; approximately 40 percent of refusals meet this definition. As shown in Column 4, the qualitative results for the transition period are again similar to those in the baseline specification. Second, we model the outcome as an indicator that takes a value of one if there are any refusals in a district-year. Again, there is a marked increase in disturbances among (former) serfs, but not state or appanage peasants, during the two-year transition period.

Our baseline specification accounts for spatial correlation in unobserved determinants of rebellion by allowing for clustering of errors at the provincial level. As an alternative approach, we estimate a model with spatial autoregressive errors (and district fixed effects) that uses an inverse-distance spatial weighting matrix. Column 6 reports the results, which are essentially unchanged from before.

There was a further reform of the state peasantry in 1866. For most provinces, the legal impact of this reform was relatively small, but mandatory redemption (i.e., purchase of land allotments) was established for state peasants in the nine western provinces affected by the Polish Rebellion that began in 1863. The same nine provinces saw substantial improvements in land allotments and redemption terms for former serfs; three of the nine provinces had also been affected by the "inventory reform" of the 1840s. To verify that these events are not biasing our estimates for the post-emancipation period, we drop all

Table 3.2 Peasant Unrest: Theft and Violence

	Baseline (1)	TsGAOR only (2)	1858–1862 (3)	Large events (4)	Binary outcome (5)	Spatial errors (6)	Drop western (7)	Weather shocks (8)
			(Former) serfs					
Transition period	0.299	0.121	0.226	0.135	0.221	0.268	0.254	0.280
	(0.044)	(0.023)	(0.045)	(0.027)	(0.028)	(0.018)	(0.035)	(0.036)
Post-emancipation period	−0.014	−0.005		0.004	−0.013	−0.028	−0.042	−0.009
	(0.015)	(0.005)		(0.006)	(0.011)	(0.011)	(0.012)	(0.020)
Provincial rye prices								−0.060
								(0.033)
			State and appanage peasants					
Transition period	−0.006	−0.005	−0.023	−0.005	−0.006	−0.005	−0.006	0.001
	(0.003)	(0.002)	(0.009)	(0.003)	(0.003)	(0.006)	(0.004)	(0.005)
Post-emancipation period	−0.001	−0.001		−0.003	−0.000	0.000	−0.001	0.001
	(0.003)	(0.003)		(0.003)	(0.003)	(0.003)	(0.004)	(0.003)
Provincial rye prices								−0.020
								(0.010)
Observations	9,849	9,849	2,345	9,849	9,849	9,849	7,959	7,529
District FEs	Yes	Yes	Yes	Yes	Yes	Yes	Yes	Yes

Notes: Linear fixed-effects models on a panel of districts in European Russia from 1851 to 1871. The outcome is number of acts of theft and violence (see text for definition), but for Model 5, where the outcome is presence of at least one such event. Models for (former) serfs and state/appanage peasants run separately. Transition period is 1861 and 1862. Model 2 restricts the analysis to events drawn from the archive TsGAOR, whereas Model 3 restricts the sample to the years 1858–1862. Model 4 considers only disturbances involving more than one village or district. Model 6 is a spatial panel fixed-effects model, implemented using the splm package in R, that models spatial autoregressive errors with an inverse-distance weighting matrix. Model 7 drops districts in nine western provinces. In parentheses, standard errors that correct for clustering at the provincial level (but for Model 6).

Table 3.3 Peasant Unrest: Rejection of Terms of Emancipation

	Binary outcome		Count	
	OLS	Spatial errors	OLS	Spatial errors
	(1)	**(2)**	**(3)**	**(4)**
Fertile soil	0.227	0.275	0.422	0.426
	(0.081)	(0.098)	(0.271)	(0.250)
Serf population,	0.420	0.434	1.446	1.450
1857 (100,000s)	(0.124)	(0.089)	(0.468)	(0.223)
Constant	−0.042	−0.051	−0.077	−0.078
	(0.015)	(0.144)	(0.050)	(0.355)
Observations	462	462	462	462
Province FEs	Yes	Yes	Yes	Yes
R^2	0.320		0.385	
Log Likelihood		−215.642		−624.208

Notes: Linear models on a cross section of districts in European Russia. The outcome is presence (Models 1 and 2) or count (Models 3 and 4) of events involving either refusals or theft and violence, 1861 and 1862, in which peasants rejected terms of emancipation. Models 1 and 3 adjust standard errors for clustering at the provincial level. Models 2 and 4 are spatial autoregressive error models, implemented using the `spdep` package in R, that use an inverse-distance weighting matrix.

observations in the provinces affected by the Polish Rebellion in Column 7; there is little change from the baseline sample.[29]

Finally, emancipation could have been more threatening to peasants whose livelihood was threatened by weather shocks. To check for this possibility, we include provincial rye price as a control variable in Column 8. There is no discernible impact of this variable, and the point estimates on the period variables are nearly identical to those in the baseline specification.[30]

Table 3.2 provides analogous estimates for events involving theft and violence. As with refusals, there is strong and consistent evidence of a sharp

---

[29]   As an additional check on outlier provinces, we drop each province in turn. The largest impact is from dropping districts in Saratov, from which the point estimate on the transition dummy for (former) serfs drops to 0.824. For thefts/violence, discussed later, the large impact is from dropping districts in Podolia, from which the analogous estimate drops to 0.269

[30]   Unfortunately, the panel of rye prices is missing observations for approximately half of the sample in 1860 and 1861. We obtain very similar point estimates – still precisely estimated – if we run the same regressions on a balanced panel.

increase in unrest among (former) serfs, but not state and appanage peasants, during the transition period.

3.5.2 Cross-Sectional Regressions

Table 3.3 validates the claim that the correlation between soil fertility and unrest involving rejection of terms of emancipation is generally robust to conditioning on the size of the former serf population, to the inclusion of province fixed effects, and to various changes in specification.

4 Other Cases

In this section we examine the generalizability of our argument beyond Imperial Russia. We do so through brief qualitative analyses of several major institutional reforms: the Tanzimat Reforms of the late Ottoman Empire; the land reform of Tiberius Gracchus (*Lex Sempronia Agraria*) in ancient Rome; the abolition of feudalism during the early days of the French Revolution; and various land reforms in twentieth-century Latin America.

Two considerations motivate our selection of these cases. Spanning two millennia and three continents, the four reforms exhibit broad temporal and spatial variation, thus reducing the risk of overgeneralization from our close analysis of Russia's emancipation of the serfs in 1861. In addition, each case provides important analytical leverage – spatial and temporal variation internal to the case, useful comparison with another case, or rich historical detail through which we can trace out mechanisms. We are thus able to identify counterfactuals and isolate the impact on rebellion of state capacity and the nature of reform, as realized through local implementation and the emergence of grievances.

Among the four historical episodes we examine, the Ottoman Empire's Tanzimat Reforms are the clearest example of a "most likely" case for our argument (e.g., Eckstein, 1975; Gerring, 2007), given their similarity to the Russian reform we examine in the previous section. Similarly to Russia's emancipation of the serfs, the Ottoman reforms were carried out by a major yet declining multiethnic and religiously heterogeneous Eurasian empire with a weak central government and limited state capacity. The two reforms overlapped temporally and were driven by the same desire to modernize the state in response to humiliating military defeats. Both reforms distributed rights and resources to previously excluded groups, and each relied heavily on local implementation by agents with a stake in the pre-reform status quo. We thus deliberately stack the deck in favor of the same outcome we observe in the Russian case. Our finding that similar mechanisms are at work permits a cautious initial optimism about the generalizability of our argument.

We then proceed to a case that exhibits important internal variation in reform implementation: the *Lex Sempronia* of Tiberius Gracchus. As in the Russian case, the reform centered on land redistribution. The reform was ultimately restricted to Roman citizens only and was implemented in maximally top-down fashion. Initially, however, the reform was also intended to benefit farmers among Rome's Italian allies. This latter attempt at redistribution was effectively blocked by local elites over which the reform commission had no legal jurisdiction; the botched redistribution was arguably among the factors that led to the outbreak of the Social War in 88 BCE.

Our third case engages in process tracing to examine a key assumption of our theoretical argument: grievances, and thus rebellion, increase to the extent that reform fails to live up to its original promise. In absolute terms, the abolition of feudalism in revolutionary France increased the welfare of the peasantry. Nonetheless, subversion by landowners left peasants far short of what they had been promised by the National Assembly just a short time before, fueling dissatisfaction and consequently unrest.

Finally, we briefly analyze several instances of land reform in twentieth-century Latin America. Although broadly similar in intent, these reforms differed greatly in the context in which they were carried out, with important variation not only across (Costa Rica, Peru, and Colombia) but also within (Peru and Chile) states. Where state capacity and reform design implied that reform was implemented as intended, land redistribution tended to promote social stability. Where that was not the case, violence followed.

4.1 The Tanzimat Reforms and Social Unrest in the Ottoman Empire

4.1.1 Analysis

The Tanzimat Reforms of the Ottoman Empire (1839–1876) are similar in numerous respects to the Great Reforms in Russia under Tsar Alexander II. Both sets of reforms were undertaken in the mid-nineteenth century by weak central governments of declining multiethnic Eurasian great powers, with a common goal of modernizing the state in the wake of humiliating defeats. Both the Ottoman and the Russian reforms granted legal rights and freedoms to previously excluded and oppressed groups, created new institutions of local governance, improved representation, and curtailed the powers of the pre-reform traditional elites (Brisku, 2017). The reforms did differ in their primary emphasis: land redistribution was the cornerstone of the reform effort in Russia from the very beginning, whereas the initial focus in the Ottoman Empire was on other issues, such as modernization of the public administration and taxation. Nonetheless, both empires suffered from state weakness and the limited capacity of the central government, and each had to delegate much of reform implementation to local elites with a stake in the pre-reform status quo. The Ottoman experience was thus predictably similar to that which we document in Russia: a watered-down implementation that sparked unrest and violence by the reforms' intended beneficiaries.

By the early nineteenth century, the Ottoman Empire was rapidly declining. A series of humiliating military defeats by external powers – first and foremost Russia – substantially reduced the state's territory. Insurgents and local strongmen in outlying provinces from Egypt to the Balkans gained de jure or de facto independence from the central government. In the Anatolian heartland of the Ottoman Empire, economic and legal institutions were antiquated and ill-equipped to cope with the challenges of the modern era. Within the state itself, tensions were building among various social and religious groups (Brisku, 2017, p. 8). The empire's very survival necessitated far-reaching reforms and fast modernization along multiple dimensions: social, military, economic, and legal.

The Tanzimat (literally "reform" or "reorganization") era began in 1839 with the accession to the throne of Sultan Abdülmecid, who would rule the empire until his death in 1861. On November 3, 1839, an imperial edict authored by the leading reformer, Foreign Minister Reşit Pasha, announced the beginning of a new period in Ottoman history. Known as the Gülhane (Rose Garden) Edict, the document outlined a radical transformation and modernization of Ottoman social, legal, economic, and military affairs.

The Gülhane Edict focused on four key changes. First, the Sultan voluntarily abrogated absolute control over his subjects' fate and introduced some legal guarantee of rights to life, honor, and property. Second, the reform abolished an antiquated tax system built on tax farming and innumerable local dues and payments, instituting in their place direct taxation and a small number of universally collected taxes. Third, the Edict envisioned a new, modern military based on conscription. Fourth and finally, the reform guaranteed equality before the law to all Ottoman subjects regardless of religion, thus ending legally enshrined discrimination against non-Muslim minorities.

An additional Reform Edict, specifying in detail the promises of the Gülhane Edict, was published in 1856 to coincide with the peace conference that concluded the Crimean War (Zürcher, 2004, pp. 52–53, 57). As a part of the broader reform effort, the Ottoman state also introduced new legal codes (including a Land Code in 1857), abolished slavery, created several modern educational institutions, carried out a census, and established a Central Bank. The reforms also sought to broaden popular participation in, and impact on, governance, thus establishing new consultative bodies at both the central and local levels. The Tanzimat era ended with the promulgation of the Ottoman Empire's first constitution in 1876 (Aytekın, 2013, p. 310).

The Tanzimat reforms were enormous in their ambition, but the central government's weak capacity and small size hindered the transition from grand intention to a new reality on the ground. This was especially true in the field of taxation, where the switch from tax farming to direct collection required the appointment of salaried tax collectors (*muhassil*) at the local level (Shaw and Shaw, 1977, p. 96; Zürcher, 2004, p. 62). By necessity, many of the newly appointed tax collectors were in fact the same local elites who had previously served as tax farmers (İnalcık, 1976, p. 11). These elites often stood to lose from the new policies – through the loss of status, personal tax exemptions, lucrative tax-farming contracts, and the provision of long-established dues and obligations from the peasantry.

John Bragg's detailed analysis of Tanzimat-era notables in the typical mid-sized Anatolian town of Tokat demonstrates the ability of a small and extremely interconnected elite to use state weakness to its advantage. The central government needed these individuals' experience, knowledge, and social capital to carry out the reforms, and Tokat's elites were given key roles in the newly created governance institutions. Officials sent by the government from outside the town were either co-opted into local elite networks or became dependent on them (Bragg, 2014, p. 50). After being given access to and influence over Tanzimat institutions, local "power brokers used the councils and courts as platforms to steer events" in a direction that would benefit them. The outcome was that "[i]n effect, the state subcontracted its reform agenda to provincial leaders" (Bragg, 2014, pp. 2, 26). Such subcontracting was clearly beneficial to the success of the reforms when the goals of the local elites and the central government were aligned, but it also gave local actors de facto veto power over implementation if reforms posed a threat. The situation in other localities was likely quite similar.

What were the effects of "subcontracting" reform to local elites? Unfortunately, we are not aware of any comprehensive countrywide data on revolts during the Tanzimat era. Nonetheless, such evidence as does exist suggests a restive population prone to disturbances (Aytekın, 2012, p. 192). Peasant unrest during the Tanzimat years was especially intense, "quite probably, the greatest of the nineteenth-century Ottoman Empire" (Quataert, 1993, p. 33; see also Aytekın, 2012, p. 192). Several well-researched cases suggest that, as in Russia, the protests and violence of the era had their roots in local elites' influence over, and at times complete hijacking of, the implementation of reform.

Among the best-studied instances of peasant unrest is the revolt in the vicinity of Vidin (contemporary Bulgaria) in 1849–1850. In the provinces, "the central government had faced serious problems created by officials who had firmly established themselves in a provincial post and wielded nearly independent authority" (Pinson, 1975, p. 103; see also Bragg, 2014, p. 1). The reforms did not change this dynamic. As in Tokat, the pre-reform Turkish elite in Vidin quickly came to dominate the newly created institutions and administration, reducing "the power of the governor to close to nothing" (İnalcık, 1976, p. 16).

The events that led to the revolt are quite similar to numerous protest events in post-Emancipation Russia. The local peasants, predominantly Christians, were subject to many special payments and obligations. One such requirement was the *angarya*, a collective labor obligation not very different from the Russian *barshchina*. The angarya was abolished throughout the Empire by the Gülhane Edict, but, with little ability on the part of the central government to enforce the ban, local authorities continued to demand it. When the peasants, who were fully aware of the reform's content, complained to the capital, local elites simply "rearranged taxation so that no real changes took place" (Pinson, 1975, p. 115).

Another area of contention was taxation. Some pre-reform taxes targeted peasants due to their religious affiliation. Others were simply arbitrary, such as the "earth money," a tax on walking on the land. But the implementation of the new, equal, and non-discriminatory tax system also encouraged grievances. Tax collectors were not subject to any meaningful oversight, and they demanded excessive taxes in violation of legal limits. Occasionally this excessive collection was carried out in collaboration with members of the local administration, including those tasked with carrying out the Tanzimat reforms (Pinson, 1975, p. 115).

Finally, local elites tried to use the reform to gain new landholdings at peasants' expense. An important component of the Tanzimat reforms was the modernization of the armed forces. Originally, the Ottoman army was territorially based and funded by revenues from land allocated by the government to members of the military, the *sipahi*. Over time, the role of the sipahi-origin class expanded from military service to participation in local administration and tax collection. In 1842, sipahi descendants agreed to return the land they held in exchange for government pensions. However, unwilling to fully relinquish the property they viewed as their own, the Vidin sipahi class moved to subvert the plan by converting state allocations into private holdings not subject to the reform. The outcome of this privatization drive was an encroachment on some Bulgarian villages' common lands (Pinson, 1975, pp. 116–117; see also Quataert, 1993, p. 35).

Naturally, these pressures led to numerous grievances among the Bulgarian peasants who had been promised more equitable taxation, the abolition of the angarya, and freedom from sipahi control. When local elites derailed these promises, the peasants had little recourse. The police were unresponsive, and the local *meclis* – a consultative institution established to provide greater representation to citizens, Muslim and non-Muslim alike – was dominated by pre-reform Turkish landlords (Aytekın, 2013, p. 317; Quataert, 1994, p. 878). The peasantry turned instead to rebellion. Multiple villages and up to 10,000 individuals took part in the insurgency (Aytekın, 2012, p. 198; İnalcık, 1976, p. 30). Notably, the rebels maintained that their actions were not directed against the reforms or the Ottoman state as such but instead "tax farmers, village landlords, constables and suchlike." Insurgent peasants refused to negotiate with local officials; they were willing to discuss their grievances only with a special envoy sent from the capital (Pinson, 1975, pp. 113–114).

Local elites' hijacking of the implementation of reform also led to disturbances in Anatolia proper – most notably in Canik, less than 100 miles from Tokat. There, the Hazinedar magnate family enjoyed substantial control over the regional administration, including tax farming (Aytekın, 2013, pp. 317–318). Similarly to the situation in Tokat, the family and its close allies were able to fully capture the local councils established as part of the reform process (Aytekın, 2012, pp. 201–202).

The move from tax farming to direct taxation presented a direct threat to the revenue streams of the Hazinedars and other elite families. Nonetheless, as in Tokat, the central government was forced to rely on the former tax farmers to collect local dues, until such time as a modern and centralized system of taxation could be established. As a result, local families tried to protect their interests by imposing on peasants "double the regular tithe and an additional tax" (Aytekın, 2013, pp. 317–318), which led to peasant grievances and tax strikes. Additionally, elite families attempted to claim peasant land and villages included in their past tax farm as private property. When the peasants protested, the local Tanzimat councils, which almost entirely consisted of the very individuals tasked with taxing the peasants, supported the elites' demands.

Notwithstanding these numerous attempts to subvert the intent of reform, the welfare of the peasants in Canik did improve – in large part because of reforms that could be centrally mandated, such as the grant of legal rights and equality before the law. At the same time, the ability of local elites to undermine the implementation of tax and other reforms opened a wedge between the promise of the Gülhane Edict and the reality for peasants across the empire. The outcome was a protracted conflict that continued until the 1880s.

"Paradoxically, the very reforms designed to create a coherent society unified by a common ideology, and ... universal, standardized laws, had the effect of exposing and deepening the fissures within the Ottoman state and society," summarizes Hanioğlu (2010, p. 107). Implementation of a substantial portion of the reform agenda by local elites with a stake in the pre-reform status quo, as the cases of Vidin and Canik demonstrate, undoubtedly contributed to this outcome.

4.1.2 Summary

As in our other case studies, we summarize the discussion by answering the key questions that guide our analysis: What was the capacity of the state and the nature of reform? How did these determine the degree of local control over reform? To what extent did local implementation "drift" from the promise of reform? And how did this affect the incidence of rebellion?

As in Russia, the Ottoman state had limited ability to project power outside of the imperial capital. The reformist government was thus forced to rely heavily on local elites, including pre-Tanzimat tax farmers and landowners, to carry out those elements of the reform agenda that could not be implemented centrally, such as tax collection. The new policies posed a direct threat to the welfare of these traditional elites. This confluence of opportunity and motive led to a substantial subversion of reform. As the cases of Vidin and Canik illustrate, the resulting gap between the promise and implementation of the Tanzimat reforms provoked rebellion among precisely those whom the central government intended to benefit.

4.2 The Land Reform of Tiberius Gracchus

4.2.1 Analysis

Land and politics have been intimately linked for millennia. One of the best-known early instances of land reform is the *Lex Sempronia Agraria* (*Lex Sempronia* for short, 133 BCE) of ancient Rome. Led by Tiberius Sempronius Gracchus, his younger brother Gaius Gracchus, and their allies, the reform aimed to redistribute public land to impoverished Romans. In contrast to the Russian case, the core of the reform was carried out centrally and did not lead to large-scale unrest among the Roman peasantry. At the same time, various accounts point to blocked implementation of the reform in areas controlled by Rome's Italian allies as among the root causes of the subsequent Social War (91–88 BCE) between Rome and its Italian neighbors.

The exact causes and consequences of the reform are subject to heated debates and competing interpretations, but the general outline of events that emerges from the historical record is quite clear. By 134 BCE, when Tiberius Gracchus was elected Tribune of the People, the Roman countryside and especially small-scale, family-based farming – "the traditional backbone of Italian agriculture" (Beard, 2015, p. 221) – were in a state of acute crisis. The situation was largely a product of Roman territorial expansion and wars of conquest. Frequent warfare and long periods of military service in the legions, to which Roman farmers were subject, took young and middle-aged males away from their land for substantial periods of time, with devastating consequences for their families' economic well-being. Moreover, the economic benefits of Roman military victories were very unequally distributed, with a small elite reaping most benefits. Money and slaves flowing to rich Romans from abroad allowed these elites to consolidate and expand their landholdings into large estates – the *latifundia* – at the expense of peasant farmers, who could not compete at small scale and against the unpaid labor of slaves (Roselaar, 2010, pp. 146–147, 223; Stockton, 1979, pp. 7–10). Hopkins (1978, p. 30) aptly summarizes this process by stating that "Roman peasant soldiers were fighting for their own displacement."

The availability and use of public land – the *ager publicus populi Romani* – widely exacerbated this process of displacement and growing rural inequality. Public land was an outcome of Rome's territorial expansion and confiscation of defeated enemies' holdings: tracts so acquired became the property of the Roman people as a whole. Nonetheless, although officially owned by the Roman state, public land was available for private use by Roman citizens. Such use was extensive but highly unequal, mostly benefiting the Roman elites who could use this land for herding and large-scale cultivation (Roselaar, 2010, pp. 1, 4). Moreover, even though the land belonged to the Roman state, in practice it was also used by Rome's Italian allies (Richardson, 1980, p. 4), many of whom owned it before Roman conquest or confiscation and continued to exploit it with Rome's tacit acquiescence (Stockton, 1979, p. 11). As Italian allies contributed to the Roman military effort and enjoyed its spoils, the Italian countryside similarly experienced consolidation of farmland and the displacement of small-scale farmers.

Many impoverished small farmers moved to Rome in search of new employment, but a substantial number remained in the countryside, destitute and struggling to eke out a living. In addition to its moral and economic dimensions, such displacement had significant national-security implications, as impoverished ex-farmers had few children and owned little property, thus becoming exempt from military service (Bernstein, 1969, p. 5; Stockton, 1979, p. 40). *Lex Sempronia* was designed to solve these problems.

The reform proposal put forward by Tiberius Gracchus built upon existing legislation, the *Lex Licinia de modo agrorum* of 367 BCE. This law, which was in practice widely ignored, limited the use of public land by private citizens to 500 *iugera* (about 125 hectares or 300 acres) (Roselaar, 2010, pp. 96, 113). Tiberius Gracchus intended to enforce the law and require individuals who used more public land than legally allowed to transfer the excess back to the state. The most innovative and radical component of Tiberius Gracchus's plan was the next step: to redistribute the land thus returned to small farmers in a manner that built upon previous Roman experience in establishing colonies and military settlements (Duncan, 2017, p. 24). As partial compensation, Roman citizens who lost land through this process would receive secure tenure rights for the 500 iugera they were initially allowed to exploit, plus an additional 250 *iugera* for each child (Richardson, 1980, p. 1).

The plan immediately faced two key obstacles. The first was the Roman state's limited capacity: the authorities did not fully know the exact boundaries and extent of the public land they owned (Roselaar, 2010, p. 116). The solution to this problem was to appoint a three-man commission that, with the assistance of land surveyors and numerous other personnel, would determine and eventually distribute the newly available public land. The original commission comprised Tiberius Gracchus himself, his younger brother Gaius Grachhus, and Appius Claudius Pulcher, Tiberius Gracchus's father-in-law (Duncan, 2017, p. 32). That such a seemingly monumental task could be carried out by such a small group is evidence of Rome's comparatively small size, by modern standards, but more importantly the consequence of established procedures now adapted to a different purpose. In its execution, land redistribution was little different from establishing colonies and military settlements. A generally weak state had capacity to centrally implement reform because the process of implementation was itself not novel.

A second, much more severe problem was the opposition to the plan in the Senate, many members of which were large landowners and hence were to lose from the reform. For generations, such individuals benefited from the excessive use of public land and mainly treated it as their private property (Roselaar, 2010, pp. 116, 238). To bypass the Senate, Tiberius Gracchus took the proposal directly to the Plebeian Assembly (*Concilium Plebis*), a highly unusual yet not unprecedented political move (Stockton, 1979, pp. 62–63). When the Assembly adopted the proposal, it became law that the Senate could not overturn.

Unable to strike down the reform entirely, the Senate then tried to stymie its implementation by not appropriating funds for the commission's work.

Frustrated, Tiberius Gracchus decided to fund the commission's activities and the land reform more broadly from a different source – the coffers of the Kingdom of Pergamum, which was bequeathed to the Roman people by the just deceased and heirless King Attalus III, a longtime Roman ally (Duncan, 2017, pp. 32–34; Watts, 2018, pp. 85–87). Tiberius Gracchus argued that, because the kingdom was given to the Roman people, he – as tribune of the people – had the authority to use its funds. This move was also a direct challenge to the Senate and its authority to govern Rome's public finances and foreign relations. The senators' alarm grew larger still when Tiberius Gracchus decided to run for reelection and seek the tribunate for another term. Although technically not illegal, it was nonetheless an extraordinary step that provoked an angry and violent reaction. During the electoral campaign, an armed mob led by key senators attacked Tiberius Gracchus and his supporters. Tiberius himself died after being brutally beaten with the legs of a bench (Duncan, 2017, pp. 35–36).

Although Tiberius Gracchus lay dead at the entrance to the Temple of Jupiter, it is unclear whether the land reform specifically, rather than his broader political ambitions and confrontation with the Senate over foreign relations, were the main drivers of the violence (Stockton, 1979, p. 69). Even after Tiberius's death the redistribution of land mostly continued as planned; Tiberius was replaced as land commissioner by one of the reform's authors (Duncan, 2017, p. 40). The commission worked "until perhaps 118 BC, though other land reform measures continued even after that date" (Watts, 2018, p. 91). According to some interpretations, wealthy Romans could find at least some consolation in receiving secure tenancy rights over their remaining allotments of public lands (e.g., Roselaar, 2010, pp. 231, 238; Stockton, 1979, pp. 41, 59); another argument suggests that powerful landowners could sometimes find ways to protect the public land they exploited from redistribution (Howarth, 1999, p. 291). Whatever the contributing factors, it is undeniable that by concentrating reform implementation in the hands of central authorities – the three-man land commission – the plan largely neutralized the danger of subversion by disgruntled local elites. Large landowners could murder Tiberius Grachhus, but the reform's design prevented it from being watered down to any great extent, at least as far as Roman citizens were concerned.

According to Roselaar, the results of the reform were "quite impressive"; the commission "achieved a very great deal within a very short time" by providing land to as many as 130,720 settlers (Roselaar, 2010, p. 252). More importantly for our purposes, the process by which the reform was carried out not only improved the welfare of these Roman citizens in absolute terms but most likely avoided disappointment when measured against the promise of reform itself.

The outcome was an apparently peaceful response among those the reform was intended to benefit.

The situation was different for Roman allies elsewhere in Italy. Here the details are murkier and more limited, yet the available information nonetheless does allow for informed speculation (but no more than that) about the impact of *Lex Sempronia* on peasants who were not Roman citizens. Some still debate whether Tiberius Gracchus planned to extend the redistribution of public land to Italian non-Romans, but many ancient accounts and recent analyses do support this suggestion (see, for example, Shochat, 1970; Richardson, 1980). At the same time, it is also clear that non-Romans were eventually denied the benefits of public land redistribution (Roselaar, 2010, pp. 244–245). Tiberius Gracchus's intention aside, distributing Roman state land to noncitizens posed a legal problem. This conundrum could have been avoided by extending Roman citizenship as well as land to Italian small farmers (Richardson, 1980), but such a proposal was a severe threat to the elites of Rome's allies. Similarly to their Roman counterparts, Italian elites were in danger of losing substantial income from land redistribution. Additionally, should their peasants become Roman citizens en masse, this would inevitably undermine the tax base and create problems for military manpower (Howarth, 1999, p. 292).

Unlike large Roman landowners, Italian elites did not have the formal tools to fight the reform plan. They fell back instead on indirect means of resistance, such as refusing to cooperate with the commission and grinding its work to a halt (Howarth, 1999, p. 292). Next, leveraging a number of land disputes between Italian landowners and the agrarian commission, in 129 BCE Italian elites used their connections to Scipio Aemilianus, a prominent Roman politician and military commander, to persuade the Senate to declare the land reform in allied territories to be a matter of foreign policy and therefore under the exclusive purview of the Senate. Tuditanus, the consul who was appointed to deal with such issues, promptly departed to lead a military campaign in the Balkans, thus removing much of the immediate threat to Italian elites' landholdings (Howarth, 1999, p. 292).

Less connected and more impoverished Italians were not so lucky. Although we cannot know their perception of the reform, it is not unreasonable to assume that, because they fought side by side with the Romans and used Roman public land for generations, they saw themselves as equally entitled to redistributed land. Duncan reports that "Tiberius himself was personally anxious about their plight, 'lamenting that a people so valiant in war, and related in blood to the Romans, were declining little by little into poverty and paucity of numbers without any hope of remedy'" (Duncan, 2017, p. 25). In that respect, the reform certainly fell below the expectations likely set by its success elsewhere.

Land-related tensions continued to simmer in Italy, generating resentment and grievances. Many Italians, especially the landless poor, felt that "their loyal behavior throughout the second century had earned them nothing" (Roselaar, 2010, p. 282). Furthermore, if previously the use of public land was an important instrument through which Rome ensured allies' acquiescence to Roman dominance, now it was largely absent, as Italian elites came to believe that eventual land expropriation was inevitable. From the perspective of Rome, it was the worst possible combination: the grievances of the poor and the fears of the elite together increased the appeal of a fight for independence. These factors contributed to the outbreak of the Social War between Rome and its former Italian allies in 91 BCE (Roselaar, 2010, pp. 281–284). This, writes Richardson of Tiberius Gracchus's land reform, "would not be the only instance of that single-minded reformer releasing forces which were to go far beyond his own somewhat limited vision" (Richardson, 1980, p. 11).

4.2.2 Summary

As with our other cases, we summarize our analysis by focusing on the capacity of the state and the nature of reform, the degree of local control, the extent to which local implementation "drifted" from the promise of reform, and the incidence of rebellion in response to any such drift.

At the time of Tiberius Gracchus, the Roman state was generally quite weak: still to come was the expansive administrative apparatus of Claudius and later emperors (Beard, 2015, pp. 408–409). Yet the process of implementation was not novel – much the same had been done to establish numerous colonies and military settlements – and the *Lex Sempronia* was carried out in highly centralized fashion, under control of a three-man commission consisting of key reformers. Numerous Roman citizens benefited from the reform as promised, and there was no apparent large-scale unrest in its wake.

The situation was quite different in areas controlled by Rome's Italian allies. There, the lack of Roman jurisdiction over Italian lands opened the door for local influence that eventually derailed redistribution. Such limited evidence as is available implies that this may have created a gap between what Italian peasants expected (and what was achieved elsewhere) and the reality of a blocked reform, thus contributing to the eventual outbreak of the Social War.

These divergent outcomes illustrate the key prediction of our theoretical model: reform is less likely to lead to rebellion when centrally implemented. Instructively, in ancient Rome it was institutional inheritance and jurisdictional authority that allowed for central implementation, not state capacity per se.

4.3 Rural Unrest and the Abolition of Feudalism in Revolutionary France

4.3.1 Analysis

The French Revolution is often perceived as driven primarily by the actions and desires of the middle and working classes of Paris (Jones, 1988, p. xi; McPhee, 2016, p. xii). This popular view overlooks the impact of the French countryside, where land relations and rural unrest played a critical role in the demise of the monarchy and during the Revolutionary period as a whole. In summer 1789, rural France experienced a wave of large-scale unrest known as the "Great Fear." These disturbances led the National Assembly to declare the abolition of feudalism in the kingdom, on August 4–11, 1789. The decisions of the National Assembly undoubtedly improved peasants' legal status and economic well-being, but they nonetheless fell short of the peasantry's stated expectations and desires in both content and implementation. The outcome was a new, larger, and more violent wave of unrest in the wake of reform.

With a population of approximately 26–28 million, of which at least two-thirds were peasants, prerevolutionary France was extremely heterogeneous when it came to land issues and social relations in the countryside (McPhee, 2016, p. 7; Moulin, 1991, p. 6). The country was "a patchwork of privilege" (McPhee, 2016, p. 1), though there were certain constants. In the years prior to the Revolution, French landlords could

> collect a variety of monetary and material payments from the peasants; could insist that nearby villagers grind their grain in the seigneurial mill, bake their bread in the seigneurial oven, press their grapes in the seigneurial winepress; could set the date of the grape harvest; could have local cases tried in his own court ... [and] take pleasures forbidden to the peasants – hunting, raising rabbits, or pigeons – in the pursuit of which pleasures the peasants' fields were sometimes devastated. (Markoff, 1996, p. 2)

Yet by the 1780s even this long list of peasant dues and obligations was not enough. A general economic crisis, high inflation, and a series of bad harvests led landlords to extract as much from peasants as they could. To achieve this, numerous seigneurs started demanding from the peasants long-overlooked or forgotten obligations or simply invented new ones, to the point that ancient privileges morphed into a "little more than a cash-racket" (McPhee, 2016, p. 55; see also Moulin, 1991, p. 14). This extraction was met with tenacious peasant resistance – typically, through evasion, various "weapons of the weak," and litigation (Cobban, 1999, p. 34; McPhee, 2016, p. 40; Moulin, 1991, p. 23). Violent peasant protests were rare prior to the revolutionary period.

This ever-increasing pressure from landlords was compounded by a severe food crisis – the consequence of bad weather and a poor harvest in 1788 – that combined to radicalize the French peasantry. This development coincided with the general crisis of the regime and the king's decision to summon the Estates-General. The elections to that body in spring 1789 present a unique window into the peasants' mindset and desires. As part of the electoral process, communities throughout the country met to compile *cahiers de doléances* – lists of grievances that were to be presented to the king. Not surprisingly, peasant *cahiers* were overwhelmingly concerned with issues of seigneurial rights, monopolies, extractions, and taxes (Markoff, 1996). The dominant narrative that emerges from a large body of such documents is unequivocal: French peasants were willing to accept a new and reformed tax system, but they strongly believed that seigneurial privileges needed to be abolished outright or at the very minimum substantially curtailed (Markoff, 1996, p. 141).

The opening of the Estates-General in May 1789 and the crisis in Paris and Versailles went hand in hand with unrest in the countryside. The state bureaucracy disintegrated in the provinces, and, as news of the storming of the Bastille and other bold moves by representatives of the Third Estate reached rural areas, the peasants braced themselves for the nobility's revenge (McPhee, 2016, pp. 74–75). The general anxiety was exacerbated by worries about a ripening harvest that at last promised to be plentiful, reversing the misery and hunger of previous years. To protect themselves and their fields from external violence, in mid-summer 1789 many peasant communities started mobilizing and forming militias (Moulin, 1991, p. 26).

Peasant mobilization and unrest were driven by a combination of fear, hope, and panic. In some regions the violence started in the spring, but by July to early August most of the country was in turmoil. Peasant mobilization quickly escalated into a massive wave of protests and attacks on landlords, their property, and symbols of status and authority, from archives to granaries to weather vanes, the latter the emblem of seigneurial courts. Geographically, the hotspots of peasant unrest correlated with the areas in which the landlords' increased extraction of duties was most pronounced (McPhee, 2016, p. 57).

This unrest, the "Great Fear" of summer 1789, greatly alarmed the legislators of the National Assembly – a new body led by Third Estate members of the Estates-General – as news of the carnage started reaching the capital. The panic in the National Assembly reached its climax on August 4. A debate that started with the intent of limiting or abolishing certain seigneurial rights quickly transformed into an "electric wind of generosity" by panicked legislators (McPhee, 2016, p. 77). The outcome was a series of simultaneously radical and incoherent resolutions adopted August 4–11.

The most famous article of the August Decree was the first, through which the National Assembly proclaimed that it "completely abolish[ed] the feudal system." Despite this ambitious and unequivocal claim, in subsequent decrees the sobered delegates also qualified and limited the promised abolition of feudalism. This was achieved by making a key conceptual distinction between two types of duties: those that derived from personal servitude and were "imposed by violence or personally degrading" and those that were related to the use and ownership of land (Moulin, 1991, p. 28). The former were abolished outright without compensation, while the latter were to be redeemed by compensating the landlords. In the meantime, these redeemable dues were to be collected as usual until a permanent settlement was reached. Equally confusing, the National Assembly abolished seignourial courts, but, given the lack of alternatives, their jurisdiction and manpower were left intact until further notice (Jones, 1988, pp. 81–82; McPhee, 2016, pp. 77–78). The decree, which did not have the power of law, was submitted for approval to the king, becoming the law of the land only on November 3, 1789.

The decree of the National Assembly was driven by fear of peasant unrest, with the aim of reducing underlying grievances. The result, however, was exactly the opposite. Instead of quieting the Great Fear, peasant unrest only increased (Tuma, 1965, p. 61). The violence quickly spread to additional regions of the country. It became more organized, bolder, and deadlier in its outcomes. A typical instance of unrest usually involved groups of 150–200 protesters, but thousands took part in the largest attacks on castles and manor houses (Ado, 1987, p. 111). Overall, from June 1788 to June 1793, 83 percent of the kingdom's Estates-General electoral districts experienced collective rural disturbances (Markoff, 1996, p. 218).

What explains why a policy aimed at aiding the peasants, fulfilling their core demands, and quieting their violence failed to produce such an outcome, leading instead to large-scale social unrest? The answer to this question shows the importance of two factors: the ability of elites with a stake in the status quo to water down ambitious reforms, and the grievances that result when reform's implementation fails to live up to its promise.

The first article of the August Decree promised to abolish the feudal regime, but ultimately many landlord privileges and peasant obligations were reclassified as stemming from private property rights, which were to be enforced and later redeemed. Why would legislators representing predominantly the Third Estate, to which the peasants themselves belonged, support such a policy? The answer lies in the split between the masses of poor peasants and the better-off rural, and especially urban, bourgeoisie (Cobban, 1999).

The majority of French belonging to the Third Estate were peasants, yet most representatives of the Third Estate in the National Assembly came from the urban middle and professional classes. This gap between town and countryside became of utmost importance when the question of land and peasant obligations came to the fore, for three reasons. First, there were philosophical and ideological differences between urban and peasant conceptions of private property. Unlike peasants, educated urbanites strongly believed that private property rights were sacred and inalienable (Ado, 1987, pp. 126–127). They were also more likely to perceive peasant dues and obligations as deriving from property rights and land ownership, without burdening themselves with questions about the origins of such ownership (Jones, 1988, p. 88).

Second and more important, by 1789 land ownership in France was not restricted to the nobility or church institutions alone. Indeed, many professionals and better-off members of the Third Estate, peasants and city dwellers alike, owned substantial tracts of land throughout the kingdom (Ado, 1987, p. 36). The abolition of personal servitude had limited impact on the "bourgeoisie of landowners" (Cobban, 1999), but a complete removal of other peasant dues and payments could substantially harm their bottom line. It is therefore hardly surprising that, when the panic of the first days of August subsided, delegates of the Third Estate, many of them landowners, worked hard to soften the blow to their interests (Moulin, 1991, p. 27).

Third, given the collapse of the central government's authority, the success of the National Assembly's reform depended upon the agreement of local landowners to abide by the decree's provisions. The landlords, however, had little to gain from the new policies and much to lose. "Once the immediate danger of agrarian insurrection had receded, seigneurs moved to retrieve what they could from the wreckage" (Jones, 1988, p. 84). Attempting to protect their income and interests, numerous landlords continued to impose dues and to demand that peasants fulfill obligations that had been abolished by the National Assembly. Often this was done with the help of courts, which were tightly controlled by members of the landowning elite and the urban upper classes – the very groups that had worked hard to limit the scope of the abolition decree. Additionally, the landlords also had full control of seigneurial courts, which in principle had been abolished but in fact were still operating. As a result, a wave of anti-peasant legal processes took place in the second half of 1789 and early 1790 (Ado, 1987, p. 132). Finally, in some parts of the country, regional bodies hostile to the National Assembly effectively sabotaged the reform and protected the landlords (Jones, 1988, p. 84).

As in Russia, the gap between the promise and reality of reform further widened because of the communication technology of the era. In a telling instance, a delegate from the Nîmes area in southern France complained that, more than three months after the original decree, many villages in his region had not yet received the exact text; "little wonder that peasants were imagining its content as they wished" (McPhee, 2016, p. 90). That many peasants spoke little or no French certainly did not help either.

The process of drafting the *cahiers* had allowed French peasants to clearly articulate and measurably define their vision of a just social order free of seigneurial exploitation. The *cahiers* thus served as a reference point against which actual outcomes could be measured. In declaring that it was "completely abolishing the feudal system," the National Assembly only cemented these expectations. The August Decree indeed improved the welfare of the peasantry in numerous ways, leaving the peasantry better off than under the pre-abolition status quo (Ado, 1987, p. 125), but in its own contradictions and in subsequent implementation it fell short of what peasants had been led to believe they could immediately achieve. The violence continued.

4.3.2 Summary

The strength and capacity of the French state were limited even before 1789 by the extremely complex web of local customs, privileges, and exemptions that characterized the monarchy, but the revolutionary upheaval led to the near collapse of state authority. The weakness of the state contributed to rebellion in two respects. It did so first by spurring the "Great Fear" in the countryside – the initial wave of unrest that provoked a panicked National Assembly to declare the end of feudalism, thus cementing a reference point against which subsequent events would be measured. It also helped to ensure that these expectations could not be met. The central government's limited capacity forced it to continue to rely on presumably abolished bodies such as seigneurial courts, while rendering impossible the monitoring of landlords to ensure that they refrained from demanding the abolished dues and obligations. It was this gap between the promise and reality of reform that led French peasants to respond to the "abolition" of feudalism with rebellion.

4.4 Land Reform and Social Unrest in Latin America

4.4.1 Analysis

From the early days of European colonization, land relations in Latin America were characterized by extreme inequality. Most land was concentrated in the hands of tiny elites of European or mixed descent, while the masses of indigenous peasants were mercilessly exploited – largely excluded from land ownership or forced to rely on small plots for subsistence (Albertus, 2015;

Thiesenhusen, 1995). A number of very limited reforms were carried out during the nineteenth and the early twentieth centuries, but governments throughout the region made few attempts to seriously address the problems of the countryside until after World War II, when pressure for change came from a few directions: violent and political action by the peasantry, the Cuban revolution, and the U.S.-led Alliance for Progress (Kay, 2001, pp. 745–746).

Despite the mounting pressure to initiate reforms, in several countries the landholding elites were able to leverage their political influence to effectively prevent the adoption or even consideration of any meaningful land redistribution plans (Albertus, 2015; Huntington, 1968, p. 389). Such stillborn reforms are interesting but outside the scope of our analysis. Instead, we focus on several reforms that were carried out and briefly illustrate their impact on social stability.

Post-WWII land reforms in Latin America were generally characterized by their top-down implementation and the rather limited involvement of local elites. As our theory predicts, reforms of this type typically did not lead to large-scale peasant unrest. For those few cases when and where local elites were allowed to influence implementation, the result was a watered-down reform that fell below peasants' expectations and increased unrest.

It is important to stress that we do not argue that centrally implemented land reforms in Latin America did not lead to unrest altogether. Indeed, land issues were and still are among the key drivers of violence throughout the region, from Brazil to Peru to Central America. Yet this violence was largely organized and carried out either by actors who were overlooked by or excluded from reform or by those who lost their income, power, and status as a result of new policies (Kay, 2001, p. 741).

An example of the former are those highland indigenous communities in Peru that came to support the armed struggle by *Sendero Luminoso* (Shining Path) against the state. With little arable land in the highlands, there was simply not enough for the state to redistribute; land reform was mostly confined to the coastal regions of the country.[31] More pertinent to our analysis is the latter category: pre-reform landed elites, who lost their political prominence and wealth as a result of land-redistribution policies. Unable to derail reform because they were excluded from its implementation, in some countries large landowners mobilized their clients and allies at home or in the United States to block change by force. Such violence does not invalidate our argument but

---

[31] Kay goes even further by arguing that "the agrarian reform cannot by itself be blamed for this violence [by Sendero Luminoso] as other factors contributed to it, such as Peru's entrenched racism and marginalisation of its indigenous population" (Kay, 2001, pp. 749–750).

presents a different, if related, mechanism that links reform to social instability. It also clearly demonstrates the inherent difficulty of distributive reform
in weak states. Delegation of implementation to local elites with a stake in
the pre-reform status quo is likely to lead to disappointment and unrest by
reform's intended beneficiaries, whereas central implementation and the exclu-
sion of local elites from the process can lead to violent pushback from those so
excluded.

The linkage between reform's central implementation and social stability is
best exemplified by the experiences of Bolivia and Costa Rica. In Costa Rica,
land reform started in earnest in 1962. Uncultivated land, land suitable for irri-
gation, *latifundia* holdings, and land suitable for cultivation but used for cattle
herding were all eligible for expropriation by the *Instituto de Tierras y Col-
onización* (ITCO), which was established to carry out the reform (Seligson,
1984, p. 30). Importantly, from its inception ITCO was an arm of the central
government and did not rely on the cooperation of local elites. After initial
attempts at redistribution and colonization, ITCO switched its focus to resolv-
ing conflicts between peasants who squatted on private and public lands and
the legal owners of those lands. As a result of these efforts, the agency granted
peasants more than 2,000 land titles over a four-year period. Even though such
activities were a far cry from a complete transformation of land relations in the
country, they still undeniably benefited many peasants and did so in a manner
that corresponded to the reform's initial design. No substantial peasant unrest
took place in the country during or in the wake of the reform.

A more ambitious but no less centralized land reform was carried out in
Bolivia. The process – spearheaded by the Revolutionary Nationalist Movement (MNR) – started in 1953, earlier than most similar Latin American efforts.
The reform was ambitious, its outcomes impressive. Prior to 1953 the majority of the Bolivian population was landless, but by 1970 almost 80 percent of
the country's land was in the hands of those who benefited from redistribution
(Lapp, 2004, p. 36). The reform, which expropriated and redistributed the land
of large estates, was explicitly designed to limit the influence of landowning
elites. The body of the central government leading redistribution was a nine-
member Agrarian Reform Board. Of these nine, three seats were reserved for
representatives of peasants and labor unions, while another member was the
minister of peasant affairs, allied with the rural poor. Decisions made by local
agents of the central government – officials who might be under the influence of
or belong to landholding elites – had to be approved centrally – by the Agrarian
Reform Board, by the National Congress, and finally by the president himself
(Lapp, 2004, p. 36). Even though this process protected the interests of MNR-
allied landlords and was used at times to punish members of the opposition,

it effectively removed any possibility that reform might be captured by local elites. As in Costa Rica, land reform in Bolivia did not lead to significant peasant unrest (Thiesenhusen, 1995).

Land reforms in Peru under Juan Velasco Alvarado and in Chile under Salvador Allende are also often viewed as key examples of top-down, state-driven, and heavy-handed redistribution policies. Although certainly true, these very centralized reforms came on the heels of earlier attempts that were more open to local pressure and hence more effectively blocked by local elites – a point to which we will return.

Velasco's "revolution from above" began in 1968 with a military coup led by a group of reformist officers. A key element of the new regime's activities was an agrarian reform that expropriated all privately held land exceeding a stipulated maximum limit, in exchange for limited compensation. Some of the expropriations were carried out by the national armed forces. Because all land that exceeded the stipulated maximum limit was to be expropriated without exception, the government did not need to rely on local agents to determine what to redistribute. It was the "national bureaucracy that assumed responsibility for land redistribution" (Cleaves and Scurrah, 1980, p. 15). Furthermore, a special Agrarian Court System (FPA) was established to deal with problems and litigation related to expropriation. In this court, writes Mayer, "landlords were treated with little sympathy." As a result, over the course of ten years the government "expropriated 15,286 properties and nine million hectares" (Mayer, 2009, pp. 19–20), the majority of which – about 38 percent of the country's total farmland – was awarded to newly established peasant cooperatives (Mason, 1998, p. 214). Although the reform did not entirely stop peasant unrest, it was effective in limiting its extent: civil conflict was less pronounced in districts that experienced extensive expropriations than in neighboring and otherwise similar districts where reform was more limited (Albertus, 2019). A later wave of land occupations in Andahuaylas is likely explained by the relative ability of local elites in that remote region to influence the process of land redistribution (Mayer, 2009, p. 24).

Velasco's land reform is among the most far-reaching in the region. Yet no less important for our purposes are the more modest reform attempts carried out by the Belaúnde administration that was swept away by the Velasco coup. This reform, which focused on strengthening small and medium-sized family-based farming, envisioned only a limited expropriation and redistribution of elites' landholdings. Yet the Belaúnde reform did not lead to any significant results, mainly due to the landowning elites' ability to locally derail expropriation, redistribution, and titling of land to new owners. Low-level officials "often 'lost' or refused to provide peasants with copies of contracts or deeds that supported their claims." Many judges in the provinces were members of the local elite, often junior sons of wealthy landowners (Cleaves and Scurrah, 1980, pp. 155–156). The slow pace of reform led to growing social tension. The fear of peasant uprisings and their potential impact on national security were among the factors that convinced Velasco and his comrades to carry out their coup (Seligmann, 1995, p. 58). The new reform under the FPA, as already discussed, was tightly controlled by the central government to remove such obstacles to implementation.

A somewhat similar process took place in Chile. Enacted in 1967 during the presidency of Eduardo Frei Montalva, Chile's reform allowed for expropriation of privately owned land for a number of reasons, the most important of which was size. On estates larger than eighty basic irrigated hectares (BIH), all land in excess of this limit was to be expropriated and later redistributed. The reform was designed to be implemented centrally by a newly established government agency, the Corporación de la Reforma Agraria (CORA), without significant involvement by local agents (Thome, 1989, pp. 191–195).

This otherwise very centralized reform nonetheless allowed for judicial oversight by civil courts, many of which were staffed by judges coming from or allied with landholding elites. The owners of expropriated estates readily used this resource to fight redistribution. Legal challenges mostly led to no more than delays in implementation (Thome, 1989, p. 199), but the cumulative effect was significant nonetheless. The reform's stated goal was to redistribute land to 100,000 peasant families over six years, yet by 1970 less than 30 percent, and according to one estimate just above 20 percent, of the intended beneficiaries had received any land (de Janvry, 1981, p. 219; Thome, 1989, p. 191). Obviously, the elites' influence in the courts was just one among several reasons for the slow progress, but it did contribute to an overall perception of failure. As peasant dissatisfaction increased, so did unrest. Worker strikes on agricultural estates jumped "from 142 in 1965 to 1,580 in 1970, and land invasions multiplied from 7 to 465" (de Janvry, 1981, p. 219). The crisis created by growing social instability also led to the election in 1970 of the socialist Salvador Allende, who intensified Frei's reforms. Allende's policies provoked an even stronger reaction among landholding elites, whose opposition was a key factor contributing to Augusto Pinochet's military coup of 1973.

The most explicit example of the linkage between local agents' control over the implementation of reform and social unrest is Colombia. The land reform in Colombia came in the wake of a brutal civil war (*La Violencia*) between the Liberal and the Conservative Parties (1948–1958) and was originally viewed as a way to reestablish the peace and the prominence of the major parties in the countryside. Later, economic and social aspects of land redistribution also began to play an important role. The 1961 reform envisioned a limited land expropriation as well as state support for colonization projects and peasant cooperatives (Zamosc, 1986, pp. 34–35). The Colombian Institute of Agrarian Reform (INCORA) was established to carry out the new policies. According to Albertus and Kaplan (2013, p. 204),

> the Agrarian Reform Committee board [part of INCORA] made high-level policy decisions. Land reform was implemented through regional project zones created by this governing board ... The board included members of the Federation of Colombian Cattle Ranchers (FEDEGAN), a precursor to right-wing paramilitary groups, as well as elected congressmen, agricultural interests, the church, and the armed forces. Peasant representation never exceeded two of the fifteen total members. As a result, landed elites were able to shape the land reform process by (1) influencing the intensity of reform; (2) shifting its emphasis from expropriation and redistribution of latifundios to legalization and titling; and (3) determining the geographical targeting of reform.

Albertus and Kaplan's (2013) analysis of guerrilla activity in the Colombian countryside clearly demonstrates the impact of local implementation on violence. Where provincial elites were able to use their influence on and participation in the reform board to dilute redistribution, the outcome was an increase in armed unrest. However, areas that were subject to the most dedicated and prolonged attention of INCORA experienced lower levels of guerrilla violence – an outcome that Albertus and Kaplan tie to the greater implementation of land reform in such regions.

4.4.2 Summary

At least on paper, all the Latin American land reforms discussed in this section were designed as centralized processes. Yet even within this set of top-down reforms there was variation in the degree to which local actors were granted control over redistribution. Costa Rica, Bolivia, and Peru under Velasco went out of their way to neutralize the potential influence of pre-reform landowning elites. In contrast, in Colombia, Peru under Belaúnde, and Chile under Frei local elites had the ability to undermine reform through their control of courts and other local institutions. As our theory predicts, there was more "drift" from reform's intent in the latter cases than the former – and consequently more unrest.

It is difficult to say how much of this variation in local control is the result of variation in state capacity. The fact that different approaches could be tried in the same country only years apart suggests that some of the difference is the consequence of choice, not constraint. At the same time, the full capacity of the state may have been more available to some actors than to others – as in Peru, where perhaps only an officer such as Velasco could mobilize the military in support of expropriation of landowning elites.

5 Conclusion

Alexis de Tocqueville famously conjectured that citizens would be most likely to rebel precisely when reform promised to change their lives for the better. Why this should be the case is not immediately obvious. On the one hand, introspection suggests that Tocqueville was likely correct in arguing – as have more recent scholars – that reform raises expectations and that unrest follows when those expectations are not fulfilled. On the other hand, the gap between expectations and the reality of reform is not fixed. Those in a position to implement reform are often those with the most to lose from rebellion.

In this short contribution to the study of reform and rebellion, we provide a microfoundation for Tocqueville's claim and thus a theory of the impact of distributive reforms on social stability. We show that reforms that are introduced centrally but implemented locally create the conditions for rebellion by driving a wedge between what citizens expect and what they receive. By setting a reference point against which local implementation falls short, reform creates grievances that may be only partially offset by improvements over the status quo. It is the failure of officials to fully internalize these grievances – a feature of any bargaining environment in which the incentive to "rebel" is driven by expressive rather than instrumental motivations – that produces the Tocqueville paradox.

At the same time, our analysis places bounds on the effect that Tocqueville describes. It is only when reform is "complicated" or state capacity is low that reform provokes rebellion. When central governments are able to push through implementation on their own, reform unambiguously reduces rebellion.

Our analysis of several important reforms, initiated over two millennia on three continents, illustrates the empirical reach of this perspective. We most closely examine Russia's emancipation of the serfs in 1861 – a case for which we have extensive micro-level data on peasant unrest before and after emancipation was announced by Tsar Alexander II. The Russian state was far too weak to implement such a complicated reform from St. Petersburg. Practical decisions about the redistribution of land rights and renegotiation of various obligations were therefore substantially delegated to the local nobility, which took advantage of its control to subvert the intent of reform. The resulting disappointment contributed to a substantial wave of unrest among former serfs across European Russia. Critically, from the perspective of identifying the cause of these disturbances, there was no similar unrest among Russia's numerous state peasants, who were not directly affected by the reform.

Our narrative analysis of four additional cases further validates our interpretation of the Tocqueville paradox. Among these, the Tanzimat Reforms of the Ottoman Empire are most similar – substantively, administratively, and temporally – to Russian emancipation. As in Russia, Ottoman reformers were forced to rely on local elites to carry out reform; as in Russia, this led to "drift" from reform's intent that fueled unrest. The *Lex Sempronia* of Tiberius Gracchus, in turn, provides an opportunity to compare the effects of centrally and locally implemented reform. When directed at Roman citizens, land reform was implemented in top-down fashion, with little apparent dissatisfaction and no evident unrest. But when applied to lands controlled by Rome's Italian allies, local elites were able to block reform, with consequences that ultimately contributed to the outbreak of the Social War in 91 BCE.

Any study of the Tocqueville paradox must examine the French Revolution itself. Our reanalysis of this case demonstrates the importance of reference points. The National Assembly's declaration that it had "completely abolish[ed]" feudalism established expectations that could not be met, particularly given the collapse of state authority in the countryside. Finally, our brief survey of several important land reforms in contemporary Latin America allows for comparison of centralized and decentralized implementation of reform, both across and within countries. Broadly speaking, Latin American reform led to rebellion among its intended beneficiaries when, and only when, local actors had the ability to block the implementation of reform.

Even as these cases illustrate the broad applicability of our argument, they highlight mechanisms not emphasized by our highly stylized model of reform and rebellion. In both Russia and France – two instances of pre-modern communication – it took time for the extent and nature of reform to become common knowledge. Until they did, peasants were free to imagine reforms even more ambitious than promised, thus creating scope for further disappointment.

The French Revolution further demonstrates the different avenues through which limited state capacity can contribute to rebellion. Not only was a weakened French state often unable to overcome resistance by local elites, but the panicked declaration of an end to feudalism was itself a response to the disintegration of the French bureaucracy in the provinces and the unrest – the "Great Fear" of 1789 – that followed.

Our reading of the history of land reform in ancient Rome and contemporary Latin America exposes the sometimes ambiguous nature of state capacity. Although the Roman state at the time of Tiberius Gracchus was generally quite weak, the process of land redistribution anticipated by the *Lex Sempronia* was sufficiently familiar – the consequence of earlier waves of colonial and military settlement – to allow for centralized implementation (where land was controlled by Roman citizens). In Latin America, in turn, the temporal proximity of centralized and decentralized reform within the same country illustrates that only certain reformers – those with control over key institutions, such as Velasco had over the military in Peru – may be able to fully mobilize state capacity.

Finally, the demise of Salvador Allende in Chile and Tiberius Gracchus in ancient Rome highlights the double-edged nature of ambitious redistribution. On the one hand, the subversion of reform's intent by local elites can lead to grievances and unrest among reform's intended beneficiaries. On the other hand, successful redistribution can create grievances among those same elites, who may possess sufficient resources to mobilize opposition at home or from abroad.

Looking beyond the particular lessons of these cases for our theoretical framework, our results imply a general need to recalibrate theories of regime change and autocratic stability. Even ignoring intertemporal commitment problems of the sort emphasized by Acemoglu and Robinson (2006), the ability of governments to buy off excluded groups should not be taken for granted. When the complexity of reform overwhelms the capacity of the state to carry it out, and the (local) agents to which implementation is tasked have a stake in the status quo, the implementation of reform will typically fall short of its promise, producing feelings of loss that encourage rebellion against those responsible. Future work can productively examine the strategic incentives of political actors who understand the paradox that reform often leads to rebellion.

Of course, reform is often initiated by political actors who have only the vaguest notion of what will follow. This suggests a final, more practical implication of our work. Policymakers would do well to heed the lessons of the cases that we examine. Reform in weak states may generate rebellion rather than social stability. In some contexts, this may simply be the price to pay for reforms that are required for other reasons. Nonetheless, if reform is not urgent, it may be optimal to invest first in state capacity. If it is, then a less ambitious design, and less sweeping promises, may help to avoid that "most dangerous time" for bad governments – when they begin to reform.

Bibliography

Acemoglu, Daron, and Robinson, James A. 2000. Why Did the West Expand the Franchise? Growth, Inequality and Democracy in Historical Perspective. *Quarterly Journal of Economics*, **115**(4), 1167–1199.

Acemoglu, Daron, and Robinson, James A. 2001. A Theory of Political Transitions. *American Economic Review*, **91**(4), 938–963.

Acemoglu, Daron, and Robinson, James A. 2006. *Economic Origins of Dictatorship and Democracy*. Cambridge: Cambridge University Press.

Acemoglu, Daron, Egorov, Georgy, and Sonin, Konstantin. 2018. Social Mobility and Stability of Democracy: Re-evaluating De Tocqueville. *Quarterly Journal of Economics*, **133**(2), 1041–1105.

Acharya, Avidit, and Grillo, Edoardo. 2017. A Behavioral Foundation for Audience Costs. Mimeo. http://stanford.edu/~avidit/audiencecosts.pdf.

Ado, Anatolii. 1987. *Krest'iane i Velikaia Frantsuzskaiia Revoliutsiia: Krest'ianskoe Dvizhenie v 1789-1794 gg.* Moscow: Izdatel'stvo Moskovskogo Universiteta.

Albertus, Michael. 2015. *Autocracy and Redistribution*. New York: Cambridge University Press.

Albertus, Michael. 2019. Land Reform and Civil Conflict: Theory and Evidence from Peru. *American Journal of Political Science*. Forthcoming.

Albertus, Michael, and Kaplan, Oliver. 2013. Land Reform as a Counterinsurgency Policy: Evidence from Colombia. *Journal of Conflict Resolution*, **57**(2), 198–231.

Alesina, Alberto, and Passarelli, Francesco. 2015. Loss Aversion in Politics. NBER Working Paper 21077. www.nber.org/papers/w21077.

Ansell, Ben, and Samuels, David. 2010. Inequality and Democratization: A Contractarian Approach. *Comparative Political Studies*, **43**(12), 1543–1574.

Aytekın, E. Attıla. 2012. Peasant Protest in the Late Ottoman Empire: Moral Economy, Revolt, and the Tanzimat Reforms. *International Review of Social History*, **57**(2), 191–227.

Aytekın, E. Attıla. 2013. Tax Revolts during the Tanzimat Period (1839–1876) and before the Young Turk Revolution (1904–1908): Popular Protest and State Formation in the Late Ottoman Empire. *Journal of Policy History*, **25**(3), 308–333.

Beard, Mary. 2015. *SPQR: A History of Ancient Rome*. New York: Liveright.

Bendor, Jonathan. 2016. Aspiration-based Models of Politics. In Krosnick, Jon A., Chiang, I-Chant A., and Stark, Tobias H. (eds.), *Political Psychology:*

New Explorations. Milton Park, Abingdon, UK: Taylor & Francis, pp. 29–60.

Bendor, Jonathan, and Meirowitz, Adam. 2004. Spatial Models of Delegation. *American Political Science Review*, **98**(2), 293–310.

Bendor, Jonathan, Diermeier, Daniel, and Ting, Michael. 2003. A Behavioral Model of Turnout. *American Political Science Review*, **97**(2), 261–280.

Benson, Brett V., Meirowitz, Adam, and Ramsay, Kristopher W. 2016. Changing Capabilities, Uncertainty, and the Risk of War in Crisis Bargaining. *Research & Politics*, **3**(3), 1–6.

Bernstein, Alvin H. 1969. *The Rural Crisis in Italy and the Lex Agraria of 133 BC*. Ph.D. thesis, Cornell University, Ithaca.

Bertrand, Jacques. 2013. *Political Change in Southeast Asia*. New York: Cambridge University Press.

Besley, Timothy. 2016. Aspirations and the Political Economy of Inequality. *Oxford Economic Papers*, **69**(1), 1–35.

Blattman, Christopher, and Miguel, Edward. 2010. Civil War. *Journal of Economic Literature*, **48**(1), 3–57.

Boix, Carles. 2003. *Democracy and Redistribution*. Cambridge: Cambridge University Press.

Brady, Nyle C., and Weil, Ray R. 2002. *The Nature and Property of Soils*. Upper Saddle River, NJ: Prentice Hall.

Bragg, John. 2014. *Ottoman Notables and Participatory Politics: Tanzimat Reform in Tokat, 1839–1876*. New York: Routledge.

Brisku, Adrian. 2017. *Political Reform in the Ottoman and Russian Empires: A Comparative Approach*. London: Bloomsbury Publishing.

Brown, J. David, Earle, John S., and Gehlbach, Scott. 2009. Helping Hand or Grabbing Hand? State Bureaucracy and Privatization Effectiveness. *American Political Science Review*, **103**(2), 264–283.

Bruce, John W, and Knox, Anna. 2009. Structures and Stratagems: Making Decentralization of Authority over Land in Africa Cost-Effective. *World Development*, **37**(8), 1360–1369.

Camerer, Colin F., Loewenstein, George, and Rabin, Matthew (eds.). 2004. *Advances in Behavioral Economics*. Princeton, NJ: Princeton University Press.

Castañeda Dower, Paul, Finkel, Evgeny, Gehlbach, Scott, and Nafziger, Steven. 2018. Collective Action and Representation in Autocracies: Evidence from Russia's Great Reforms. *American Political Science Review*, **112**(1), 125–147.

Castañeda Dower, Paul and Markevich, Andrei. 2017. The Stolypin Reform and Agricultural Productivity in Late Imperial Russia. Mimeo. https://papers.ssrn.com/sol3/papers.cfm?abstract_id=2361860.

Chong, Dennis. 2014. *Collective Action and the Civil Rights Movement*. Chicago, IL: University of Chicago Press.

Cleaves, Peter S., and Scurrah, Martin J. 1980. *Agriculture, Bureaucracy, and Military Government in Peru*. Ithaca, NY: Cornell University Press.

Cobban, Alfred. 1999. *The Social Interpretation of the French Revolution*. New York: Cambridge University Press.

Davies, James C. 1962. Toward a Theory of Revolution. *American Sociological Review*, **27**(1), 5–19.

de Janvry, Alain. 1981. *The Agrarian Question and Reformism in Latin America*. Baltimore, MD: Johns Hopkins University Press.

de Tocqueville, Alexis. 2002 [1835/40]. *Democracy in America*. Chicago, IL: University of Chicago Press.

de Tocqueville, Alexis. 2008 [1856]. *The Ancien Régime and the Revolution*. New York: Penguin Classics.

de Tocqueville, Alexis. 2011 [1856]. *The Ancien Régime and the French Revolution*. New York: Cambridge University Press.

DellaVigna, Stefano. 2009. Psychology and Economics: Evidence from the Field. *Journal of Economic Literature*, **47**(2), 315–372.

Dennison, Tracy. 2011. *The Institutional Framework of Russian Serfdom*. New York: Cambridge University Press.

Dewatripont, Mathias, and Roland, Gérard. 1992. Economic Reform and Dynamic Political Constraints. *Review of Economic Studies*, **59**(4), 703–730.

Dewatripont, Mathias, and Roland, Gérard. 1995. The Design of Reform Packages under Uncertainty. *American Economic Review*, **85**(5), 1207–1223.

Dimitrov, Martin. 2013. *Why Communism Did Not Collapse: Understanding Authoritarian Regime Resilience in Asia and Europe*. New York: Cambridge University Press.

Domar, Evsey D. 1970. The Causes of Slavery or Serfdom: A Hypothesis. *The Journal of Economic History*, **30**(1), 18–32.

Domar, Evsey D., and Machina, Mark J. 1984. On the Profitability of Russian Serfdom. *The Journal of Economic History*, **44**(4), 919–955.

Dubow, Saul. 2014. *Apartheid, 1948–1994*. Oxford: Oxford University Press.

Duncan, Mike. 2017. *The Storm before the Storm: The Beginning of the End of the Roman Empire*. New York: PublicAffairs Books.

Dunning, Thad. 2008. *Crude Democracy: Natural Resource Wealth and Political Regimes*. New York: Cambridge University Press.

Easley, Roxanne. 2002. Opening Public Space: The Peace Arbitrator and Rural Politicization, 1861–1864. *Slavic Review*, **61**(4), 707–731.

Eckstein, Harry. 1975. Case Studies and Theory in Political Science. In Greenstein, Fred I., and Polsby, Nelson W. (eds), *Handbook of Political Science, Volume 7*. Reading, MA: Addison-Wesley, pp. 94–137.

Evtuhov, Catherine. 2011. *Portrait of a Russian Province*. Pittsburgh, PA: University of Pittsburgh Press.

Fearon, James D. 1995. Rationalist Explanations for War. *International Organization*, **49**(3), 379–414.

Field, Daniel. 1976. *Rebels in the Name of the Tsar*. Boston, MA: Houghton Mifflin.

Finkel, Evgeny, and Gehlbach, Scott. 2018. The Tocqueville Paradox: When Does Reform Prevent Rebellion? Mimeo. https://papers.ssrn.com/sol3/papers.cfm?abstract_id=3202013.

Finkel, Evgeny, Gehlbach, Scott, and Olsen, Tricia D. 2015. Does Reform Prevent Rebellion? Evidence from Russia's Emancipation of the Serfs. *Comparative Political Studies*, **48**(8), 984–1019.

Gailmard, Sean, and Patty, John. 2012. Formal Models of Bureaucracy. *Annual Review of Political Science*, **15**, 353–377.

Gandhi, Jennifer, and Przeworski, Adam. 2006. Cooperation, Cooptation, and Rebellion under Dictatorship. *Economics and Politics*, **18**(1), 1–26.

Gehlbach, Scott. 2008. What Is a Big Bureaucracy? Reflections on *Rebuilding Leviathan* and *Runaway State-Building*. *Czech Sociological Review*, **44**(6), 1189–1197.

Gehlbach, Scott, Sonin, Konstantin, and Svolik, Milan. 2016. Formal Models of Nondemocratic Politics. *Annual Review of Political Science*, **19**, 565–84.

Gerring, John. 2007. Is There a (Viable) Crucial-Case Method? *Comparative Political Studies*, **40**(3), 231–253.

Gerschenkron, Alexander. 1965. Agrarian Policies and Industrialization in Russia 1861–1917. *The Cambridge Economic History of Europe*, **6**(2), 706–800.

Grieder, Peter. 2012. *The German Democratic Republic*. New York: Palgrave Macmillan.

Grillo, Edoardo. 2016. The Hidden Cost of Raising Voters' Expectations: Reference Dependence and Politicians' Credibility. *Journal of Economic Behavior & Organization*, **130**, 126–143.

Gurr, Ted R. 1970. *Why Men Rebel*. Princeton, NJ: Princeton University Press.

Haggard, Stephan, and Kaufman, Robert R. 1992. *The Politics of Economic Adjustment: International Constraints, Distributive Conflicts, and the State*. Princeton, NJ: Princeton University Press.

Haggard, Stephan, and Kaufman, Robert R. 1995. *The Political Economy of Democratic Transitions*. Princeton, NJ: Princeton University Press.

Hanioğlu, M. Şükrü. 2010. *A Brief History of The Late Ottoman Empire*. Princeton, NJ: Princeton University Press.

Hart, Oliver, and Holmstrom, Bengt. 2010. A Theory of Firm Scope. *Quarterly Journal of Economics*, **125**(2), 483–513.

Hart, Oliver, and Moore, John. 2008. Contracts as Reference Points. *Quarterly Journal of Economics*, **123**(1), 1–48.

Healy, Andrew, Kosec, Katrina, and Mo, Cecilia Hyunjung. 2017. Economic Development, Mobility, and Political Discontent: An Experimental Test of Tocqueville's Thesis in Pakistan. *American Political Science Review*, **111**(3), 605–621.

Hoch, Steven L. 1989. *Serfdom and Social Control in Russia: Petrovskoe, a Village in Tambov*. Chicago, IL: University of Chicago Press.

Hoch, Steven L. 1991. The Banking Crisis, Economic Reform, and Economic Development in Russia, 1857–1861. *American Historical Review*, **96**(3), 795–820.

Hoch, Steven L. 2004. Did Russia's Emancipated Serfs Really Pay Too Much for Too Little Land? Statistical Anomalies and Long-Tailed Distributions. *Slavic Review*, **63**(2), 247–274.

Hopkins, Keith. 1978. *Conquerors and Slaves*. New York: Cambridge University Press.

Howarth, Randall S. 1999. Rome, the Italians, and the Land. *Historia: Zeitschrift fur Alte Geschichte*, **48**(3), 282–300.

Huber, John D., and McCarty, Nolan. 2004. Bureaucratic Capacity, Delegation, and Political Reform. *American Political Science Review*, **98**(3), 481–494.

Humphreys, Macartan, and Weinstein, Jeremy M. 2008. Who Fights? The Determinants of Participation in Civil War. *American Journal of Political Science*, **52**(2), 436–455.

Huntington, Samuel P. 1968. *Political Order in Changing Societies*. New Haven, CT: Yale University Press.

İnalcık, Halil. 1976. *Application of the Tanzimat and its Social Effects*. Lisse: Peter De Ridder Press.

Ivanov, Leonid (ed.). 1964. *Krest'ianskoe Dvizhenie v Rossii v 1861-1869 gg.: Sbornik Dokumentov*. Moscow: Mysl'.

Javeline, Debra. 2003a. *Protest and the Politics of Blame: The Russian Response to Unpaid Wages*. New York: Cambridge University Press.

Javeline, Debra. 2003b. The Role of Blame in Collective Action: Evidence from Russia. *American Political Science Review*, **97**(1), 107–121.

Jones, Peter M. 1988. *The Peasantry in the French Revolution*. New York: Cambridge University Press.

Kahneman, Daniel, and Tversky, Amos. 1979. Prospect Theory: An Analysis of Decision under Risk. *Econometrica*, **47**(2), 263–291.

Kahneman, Daniel, Knetsch, Jack L., and Thaler, Richard H. 1990. Experimental Tests of the Endowment Effect and the Coase Theorem. *Journal of Political Economy*, **98**(6), 1325–1348.

Kay, Cristóbal. 2001. Reflections on Rural Violence in Latin America. *Third World Quarterly*, **22**(5), 741–775.

Khristoforov, Igor'. 2011. *Sud'ba Reformy: Russkoe krest'ianstvo v pravitel'stvennoi politike do i posle otmeny krepostnogo prava (1830-1890-e gg.)*. Moscow: Sobranie.

Kimerling Wirtschafter, Elise. 2008. *Russia's Age of Serfdom: 1649–1861*. Malden, MA: Blackwell Publishers.

Knetsch, Jack L. 1989. The Endowment Effect and Evidence of Nonreversible Indifference Curves. *American Economic Review*, **79**(5), 1277–1284.

Kőszegi, Botond, and Rabin, Matthew. 2006. A Model of Reference-Dependent Preferences. *Quarterly Journal of Economics*, **121**(4), 1133–1165.

Lapp, Nancy. 2004. *Landing Votes: Representation and Land Reform in Latin America*. London: Palgrave Macmillan.

Lockwood, Ben, and Rockey, James. 2015. Negative Voters: Electoral Competition with Loss-Aversion. Mimeo. www.le.ac.uk/economics/ research/RePEc/lec/leecon/dp15-15.pdf.

Markevich, Andrei, and Zhuravskaya, Ekaterina. 2018. The Economic Effects of the Abolition of Serfdom: Evidence from the Russian Empire. *American Economic Review*, **108**(4–5), 1074–1117.

Markoff, John. 1996. *Abolition of Feudalism: Peasants, Lords, and Legislators in the French Revolution*. University Park, PA: Penn State University Press.

Mason, T. David. 1998. 'Take Two Acres and Call Me in the Morning': Is Land Reform a Prescription for Peasant Unrest? *The Journal of Politics*, **60**(1), 199–230.

Mayer, Enrique. 2009. *Ugly Stories of The Peruvian Agrarian Reform*. Durham, NC: Duke University Press.

McPhee, Peter. 2016. *Liberty or Death: The French Revolution*. New Haven, CT: Yale University Press.

Miller, Michael K. 2013. Electoral Authoritarianism and Democracy: A Formal Model of Regime Transitions. *Journal of Theoretical Politics*, **25**(2), 153–181.

Mo, Cecilia Hyunjung. 2018. Perceived Relative Deprivation and Risk: An Aspiration-Based Model of Human Trafficking Vulnerability. *Political Behavior*, **40**(1), 247–277.

Moon, David. 2001a. *The Abolition of Serfdom in Russia.* New York: Longman.

Moon, David. 2001b. The Inventory Reform and Peasant Unrest in Right-Bank Ukraine in 1847–48. *The Slavonic and East European Review*, **79**(4), 653–697.

Moulin, Annie. 1991. *Peasantry and Society in France since 1789.* New York: Cambridge University Press.

Oberschall, Anthony. 1995. *Social Movements: Ideologies, Interests, and Identities.* New Brunswick, NJ: Transaction Publishers.

Okun', Semen (ed.). 1962. *Krest'ianskoe Dvizhenie v Rossii v 1850–1856 gg.: Sbornik Dokumentov.* Moscow: Izdatel'stvo sotsial'no-ekonomicheskoi literatury.

Okun', Semen, and Sivkov, Konstantin (eds.). 1963. *Krest'ianskoe Dvizhenie v Rossii v 1857–mae 1861 gg.: Sbornik Dokumentov.* Moscow: Izdatel'stvo sotsial'no-ekonomicheskoi literatury.

Olson, Mancur. 1965. *The Logic of Collective Action: Public Goods and the Theory of Groups.* Cambridge, MA: Harvard University Press.

Passarelli, Francesco, and Tabellini, Guido. 2017. Emotions and Political Unrest. *Journal of Political Economy*, **125**(3), 903–946.

Pinson, Mark. 1975. Ottoman Bulgaria in the First Tanzimat Period: The Revolts in Nish (1841) and Vidin (1850). *Middle Eastern Studies*, **11**(2), 103–146.

Przeworski, Adam. 2009. Conquered or Granted? A History of Suffrage Extensions. *British Journal of Political Science*, **39**(2), 291–321.

Pushkarev, Sergei G. 1968. The Russian Peasants' Reaction to the Emancipation of 1861. *Russian Review*, **27**(2), 199–214.

Quataert, Donald. 1993. *Workers, Peasants, and Economic Change in the Ottoman Empire, 1730–1914.* Istanbul: Isis Press.

Quataert, Donald. 1994. The Age of Reforms, 1812–1914. In İnalcık, Halil, and Quataert, Donald (eds.), *An Economic and Social History of the Ottoman Empire, Volume II.* New York: Cambridge University Press.

Rabin, Matthew. 1993. Incorporating Fairness into Game Theory and Economics. *American Economic Review*, **83**(5), 1281–1302.

Rauch, James E., and Evans, Peter. 2000. Bureaucratic Structure and Bureaucratic Performance in Less Developed Countries. *Journal of Public Economics*, **75**(1), 49–62.

Richardson, John S. 1980. The Ownership of Roman Land: Tiberius Gracchus and the Italians. *The Journal of Roman Studies*, **70**, 1–11.

Robertson, Graeme B. 2011. *The Politics of Protest in Hybrid Regimes: Managing Dissent in Post-Communist Russia.* New York: Cambridge University Press.

Roselaar, Saskia T. 2010. *Public Land in the Roman Republic: A Social and Economic History of Ager Publicus in Italy, 396–89 BC*. Oxford: Oxford University Press.

Rosenbaum, Paul R. 1984. The Consquences of Adjustment for a Concomitant Variable that Has Been Affected by the treatment. *Journal of the Royal Statistical Society. Series A (General)*, 656–666.

Schiavo-Campo, Salvatore, de Tommaso, Giulio, and Mukherjee, Amitabha. 1997. *An International Statistical Survey of Government Employment and Wages*. World Bank Policy Research Working Paper 1806.

Scott, James C. 1976. *The Moral Economy of the Peasant: Rebellion and Subsistence in Southeast Asia*. New Haven, CT: Yale University Press.

Seligmann, Linda J. 1995. *Between Reform and Revolution: Political Struggles in the Peruvian Andes, 1969–1991*. Stanford, CA: Stanford University Press.

Seligson, Mitchell A. 1984. Implementing Land Reform: The Case of Costa Rica. *Managing International Development*, **1**(2), 29–46.

Shadmehr, Mehdi. 2014. Mobilization, Repression, and Revolution: Grievances and Opportunities in Contentious Politics. *Journal of Politics*, **76**(3), 621–635.

Shaw, Stanford J., and Shaw, Ezel Kural. 1977. *History of the Ottoman Empire and Modern Turkey: Volume 2*. New York: Cambridge University Press.

Shochat, Yanir. 1970. The 'Lex Agraria' of 133 BC and the Italian Allies. *Athenaeum*, **48**, 25–45.

Skocpol, Theda. 1979. *States and Social Revolutions: A Comparative Analysis of France, Russia, and China*. New York: Cambridge University Press.

Spillane, James P. 2000. Cognition and Policy Implementation: District Policymakers and the Reform of Mathematics Education. *Cognition and Instruction*, **18**(2), 141–179.

Starr, Frederick S. 2015. *Decentralization and Self-government in Russia, 1830–1870*. Princeton, NJ: Princeton University Press.

Stockton, David. 1979. *The Gracchi*. Oxford: Clarendon Press.

Stokes, Susan C. 1995. *Cultures in Conflict: Social Movements and the State in Peru*. Berkeley: University of California Press.

Svolik, Milan. 2012. *The Politics of Authoritarian Rule*. New York: Cambridge University Press.

Tarrow, Sidney. 1989. *Struggle, Politics, and Reform: Collective Action, Social Movements and Cycles of Protest*. Ithaca, NY: Cornell University Center for International Studies.

Tarrow, Sidney. 2011. *Power in Movement: Social Movements and Contentious Politics (Third Edition)*. New York: Cambridge University Press.

Thaler, Richard H. 1980. Toward a Positive Theory of Consumer Choice. *Journal of Economic Behavior & Organization*, **1**(1), 39–60.

Thiesenhusen, William C. 1995. *Broken Promises: Agrarian Reform and the Latin American Campesino.* Boulder, CO: Westview Press.

Thome, Joseph R. 1989. Law, Conflict, and Change: Frei's Law and Allende's Agrarian Reform. In Thiesenhusen, William C. (ed.), *Searching for Agrarian Reform in Latin America.* Boston, MA: Unwin Hyman, pp. 188–215.

Ting, Michael M. 2011. Organizational Capacity. *Journal of Law, Economics, and Organization*, **27**(2), 245–271.

Tsentr Ekonomicheskikh i Politicheskikh Reform. 2018. *Rost protestnoi aktivnosti naseleniia: Resul'taty vserossiiskogo monitoringa 2017–2018 gg.* http://cepr.su/2018/11/08/protests-2017-2018.

Tuma, Elias H. 1965. *Twenty-Six Centuries of Agrarian Reform: A Comparative Analysis.* Berkeley: University of California Press.

Ust'iantseva, N. 1992. Institut Mirovykh Posrednikov v Krest'ianskoi Reforme. Pages 166–183 of: Zakharova, Larisa, Eklof, Ben, and Bushnell, John (eds), *Velikie Reformy v Rossii: 1856–1874.* Moscow: Izdatel'stvo Moskovskogo Universiteta.

van Zomeren, Martijn, Spears, Russell, Fischer, Agneta H., and Leach, Colin Wayne. 2004. Put Your Money Where Your Mouth Is! Explaining Collective Action Tendencies Through Group-Based Anger and Group Efficacy. *Journal of Personality and Social Psychology*, **87**, 649–664.

van Zomeren, Martijn, Leach, Colin Wayne, and Spears, Russell. 2012. Protesters as "Passionate Economists": A Dynamic Dual Pathway Model of Approach Coping with Collective Disadvantage. *Personality and Social Psychology Review*, **16**(2), 180–199.

Volin, Lazar. 1943. The Russian Peasant and Serfdom. *Agricultural History*, **17**(1), 41–61.

Watts, Edward J. 2018. *Mortal Republic: How Rome Fell into Tyranny.* New York: Basic Books.

Wood, Elisabeth Jean. 2003. *Insurgent Collective Action and Civil War in El Salvador.* New York: Cambridge University Press.

Zaionchkovskii, Petr. 1968. *Otmena Krepostnogo Prava v Rossii.* 3rd edn. Moscow: Prosveshchenie.

Zaionchkovskii, Petr, and Paina, Esfir' (eds.). 1968. *Krest'ianskoe Dvizhenie v Rossii v 1870–1880 gg.: Sbornik Dokumentov.* Moscow: Nauka.

Zamosc, Leon. 1986. *The Agrarian Question and the Peasant Movement in Colombia: Struggles of the National Peasant Association, 1967–1981.* New York: Cambridge University Press.

Zürcher, Erik J. 2004. *Turkey: A Modern History.* London: IB Tauris.

Acknowledgments

We are grateful first and foremost to Tricia Olsen – our partner and coauthor on the 2015 article on reform and rebellion that was the genesis of this project. For comments on the work specific to this Element, we thank Avi Acharya, Kate Baldwin, Chris Blattman, Paul Castañeda Dower, John Earle, Jennifer Gandhi, Bob Gibbons, Florian Hollenbach, Otto Kienitz, Gabriel Leon, Mike Miller, Steve Nafziger, Monika Nalepa, Jack Paine, Chris Price, Emily Sellars, Mehdi Shadmehr, Konstantin Sonin, David Weimer, and four anonymous referees; participants in the annual meetings of APSA, ASEEES, SIOE, and SPSA; and participants in seminars at Chicago, the University of Chicago Center in Paris, Colorado, NYU, Stanford, Texas A&M, UC Berkeley, Virginia, Wisconsin, and Yale. Mike Duncan played a critical role in getting us up to speed on ancient Rome, and David Stasavage was cheerfully encouraging from start to finish. Gabriel Martinez, Anton Shirikov, and Julian Waller all provided excellent research assistance. Gehlbach acknowledges the financial support of the William F. Vilas Trust Estate through the Office of the Provost, University of Wisconsin – Madison.

Cambridge Elements ☰

Political Economy

David Stasavage
New York University
David Stasavage is Julius Silver Professor in the Wilf Family Department of Politics at New York University. He previously held positions at the London School of Economics and at Oxford University. His work has spanned a number of different fields and currently focuses on two areas: development of state institutions over the long run and the politics of inequality. He is a member of the American Academy of Arts and Sciences.

About the Series

The Element Series Political Economy provides authoritative contributions on important topics in the rapidly growing field of political economy.
Elements are designed so as to provide broad and in-depth coverage combined with original insights from scholars in political science, economics, and economic history. Contributions are welcome on any topic within this field.

Cambridge Elements ☰

Political Economy

Elements in the Series

A full series listing is available at: www.cambridge.org/EPEC

Printed in the United States
By Bookmasters